*This book is a gift
in memory of*

Alice Barham

The Sacramento

A Transcendent River

Storm clouds. Bob Madgic.

The Sacramento

A Transcendent River

Bob Madgic

and Walt Simmons

RIVER BEND BOOKS
ANDERSON, CALIFORNIA, 2013

ISBN 978-0-9882711-0-4 (hardcover)
ISBN 978-0-9882711-1-1 (paperback)

Published by River Bend Books
6412 Clear View Drive
Anderson, California 96007

Book Design: Eric Larson, Studio E Books, Santa Barbara
Front cover photo: Garry Bagula
Back cover photo: Marcel Siegle

First Printing, 2012

Transcend: To rise above or go beyond the limits;

to triumph over the negative or restrictive aspects;

to outstrip or outdo in some attribute, quality,

or power.

Transcendent: Exceeding usual limits; surpassing;

extending or lying beyond the limits of ordinary

experience.

This book is dedicated to those individuals who have worked and continue to work for the preservation and restoration of the Sacramento River.

Acknowledgments

One person especially shaped this book and to whom I am deeply indebted—Gayle Wattawa. I also wish to cite the immeasurable contributions of Walt Simmons on all facets of this project. I am highly thankful to Malcolm Margolin of Heyday for his early encouragement, Eric Larson for his design talents and other superb project guidance, and Candace Brown for her editing contributions. Other contributors in no particular order include: Mike Peters, Chadd Santerre, Doug Killam, Bruce King, Dave Feliz, Kevin Niemela, Mike Berry, Dennis Freeman, Caleen Sisk, Patrick O'Connell, Allan Craig, Marc Dadigan, Bobby Barrack, Steve and Suzanne Turek, Kelly Williams, John and Karen Little, Terry Grosz, Julia Cronin, Tim Palmer, Jim, Mary, and James Rickert, Garry Bagula, Joseph Silveira, Allen Harthorn, Kathleen Gilman, Gregg Werner, Gary Manies, Dawn Garcia, Jamie Patrick, Steve Evans, Mike Michalak, Sandy Hayes, Marilyn Gittings, Scott McReynolds, Dottie Smith, Diane Strachan, Byron Leydecker, Tom Weseloth, Doreeta Domke, Susan Kirstein, Bob Kinkead, Buck Grochel, Oren Nardi, Wade Sinnen, Elisha Ryan, Alex Breitler, Garth Schmeck, Mary Provence, Brigitte Schueling, Mary Jensen, Pat Tucker, Reda Thompson, Sara Sundquist, Jeff Worthington, Peggy Rebol, Lance Law, Dianna Thrasher, Paul Krafel, Dick Johnson, Barbara J. Cross, Bev Stupek, Chris Stromness, Mike Wolder, Ryan Teubert, Ben Miles, Mike Warren, Judy and Lee Salter, Michael Caranci, Sharon Paquin-Gilmore, Phil Pezzaglia, Troy Swauger, Ryan Teubert, Kelly Maroney, Dr. Eric Ritter, Robin Singler, Harry Morse, Tami L. Corn, Sheri Harral, Marti and Carl Weidert, Darlene Brown, Eric Bergren, David Carle, Ben Sacks, Joe Ferreira, John Gantner, Ellen Gentry, Greg Mensik, David Barberi, Mike Ford, Duane Little, William Vanderwaal, Virginia Siemens, Hugh Jones, Bob Castner, Ken DeCamp, Margaret Dalrymple, Koll Buer, Egon Harrasser, Brian Kreb, David Schumacher, Richard May, Robin Schrock, Michael J. Miller, Eric Bergren, Craig Nielsen.

Other important teammates were sons Kirk and Doug and daughter Jennifer—whether present in my thoughts or as river companions. Lastly, the one person who was with me and supported me the entire way, as always, is my wife Diane.

Contents

The Sacramento

A Transcendent River

Preface

My LOVE OF RIVERS IS DEEP AND ENDURing. From boyhood days spent on the Housatonic River in Connecticut to decades of family camping, rafting, and fishing outings on Sierra Nevada rivers—Stanislaus, Mokelumne, Tuolumne—they have been central to my life.

What inspired me to move from the San Francisco Bay Area to Shasta County after a career in public education was the Sacramento River. My wife, Diane, and I live in a home overlooking this magnificent waterway. The river's daily gifts are immeasurable. Constant yet ever-changing motion, myriad birds, stunning sunsets that tint the water red, and full moons that coat the surface silver are joined by a continual symphony of river sounds. I can walk to the water any time and possibly hook a spirited rainbow trout. We are truly blessed.

Rivers are indeed special. Beyond personal appreciation, few parts of the planet are as crucial to its health and that of all its creatures as free-flowing rivers. They create and sustain complex networks of living organisms. They make the earth function.

But a river is also there to nurture and refurbish the human spirit. Since the beginning, people have drawn upon the power of moving water for personal growth and recreation. Norman Maclean, author of *A River Runs Through It*, states, "A river has so many things to say that it is hard to know what it says to each of us."

A river heals. Its power to restore itself is unequaled. Freed to be themselves, rivers across the country long considered "dead" from poisonous chemicals now flow clean again. Such healing powers transfer to humans. Immersing oneself in clean, flowing water refreshes the body. Watching moving water soothes the soul. A river knows where it is going, and that certainty reassures the observer, especially one harboring doubts about his or her own direction.

The constancy of movement is transfixing. Observe water swirling or cascading over rocks, or even where the current is barely perceptible, and the repetitive pattern can be calming. A youth named Siddhartha in the book of the same name expressed his search for self-knowledge by observing water: "But today he only saw one of the river's secrets, one that gripped his soul. He saw that the water continually flowed and flowed and yet it was always there; it was always the same and yet every moment it was new. Who could understand, conceive of this? He did not understand it; he was only aware of a dim suspicion, a faint memory, divine voices."

A river bestows countless gifts. It may simply be the glimpse of a wild creature. Such a sighting reveals life's wonders and intimate connections. Images can be photographed, by the mind if not a camera: an osprey hovering high above the surface, keying on an unsuspecting fish in the water's depths; a red-tailed hawk seemingly frozen on a branch as its keen eyes search grasses below; a coyote prowling about, desperate for its next kill; a bevy of otters undulating in currents as though frolicking; cormorants with spread wings striking artistic poses on exposed rocks; a salmon suddenly breaking the surface and leaping in the air; a bald eagle gracefully flying up the river corridor; a shimmering white egret statuesquely fixed in the river's shallows; a cluster of deer ambling near the shore to quench their thirst.

What swims in the water's depths? This query has long seduced the sportsman, who with each cast of his bait or lure wonders what he might catch.

A river's currents reflect the past. One can look at the Sacramento River and visualize what once happened by its shores and in the river itself. Native American villages occupied stretches, salmon were caught, game was hunted, battles waged. A piece of land is called "Bloody Island," another "Massacre Flat." What happened there? Logs from sawmills were bolted together and floated downriver, navigated by "river rats." Paddle-wheel steamboats transported passengers up and down to fledgling river towns.

Memories can be personal. In her book *Riverwalking*, Kathleen Dean Moore writes: "The river carries a history of the land and the people who live on the land, stories collected from a thousand feeder streams and recorded in pockets of sand, in the warm and cold currents, the smell of the water, the mayflies. The river carries my own history, swirls of silt lifted by my passage, memories so thick and slippery that I struggle to keep my feet."

Like Moore, most people surely have some connection to a river. Or, as singer Roberta Flack said, "There's a river somewhere that flows through the lives of everyone."

This is certainly true for my wife and me. In retirement we chose to live alongside one of the great rivers of the world, the Sacramento. And we reap its untold benefits every day. We also know that the collective water requirements of those downstream, human or otherwise, already exceed that which is passing by. So these flows are precious. If allowed to, we believe the Sacramento will do what's right.

The Sacramento's overall importance to California and the nation is undeniable. Many look to its water to irrigate crops and quench the thirst of a massive, growing population. Others desperately seek to protect and restore parts of the river's natural character. Hanging in the balance is the Sacramento's delicate ecology, severely impacted by more than a century of human intrusions. With water being one of the most critical and contentious resources, it's crucial that citizens know and understand this river, and how changes in it can profoundly impact the natural world, including humankind.

Despite its vital significance, no major publication has yet been produced on the Sacramento River. This void—combined with my devotion to rivers generally, but especially to this waterway—prompted me to undertake this book project. It has been the most challenging of personal endeavors, for I soon realized I was dealing with many of the biggest and thorniest issues facing Californians today.

In starting on this book, I knew at once what my primary focus would be—the power and beauty of the natural Sacramento River, including the flora and fauna that co-exist with it. It's true, of course, that the river has been dramatically altered, mainly by dams, levees, and diversions. One has to accept that the Sacramento will never be a complete natural system again. But humankind has learned that there are no substitutes, no technological fixes, which sustain the health of the planet better than nature functioning on its own terms. To the degree possible, this is the path that should be taken with the Sacramento. Many individuals and organizations—"river champions"—have worked and continue to work for this crucial priority.

The book's second major theme is the countless ways the Sacramento contributes to people. The two themes go hand-in-hand: the more the river is allowed to be itself, the more it has to offer humans. Many such returns are fully doc-

umentable, like recreational and economic opportunities. Some are not. How does a person measure the inestimable value of having salmon in a river? Or the peace and tranquility a river offers to whoever partakes of its flows? We cannot. We only know deep and irreplaceable loss when they are gone.

These themes are conveyed in this book's title. For despite countless alterations to its flow and compromises to its character, the Sacramento River transcends such degradations to foster and sustain life. It is imperative that it continue to do so.

—Bob Madgic
Anderson, California

Rippling water. Bob Madgic.

Author's evening visit to the river. Allan Craig.

Prologue

THE RIVER CURRENT WHERE I STAND IS mesmerizing. The tapestry is one of constant movement, yet it's always the same. Even the gushes of white water where the river tumbles over ledges and rocks present recurrent patterns and a repetitive melody.

But it's an interruption to the river's constancy that I look for this evening.

Moments pass. Then my practiced eye glimpses the variation I seek. In an almost indistinguishable dissimilarity, the surface plane is broken by a fish stabbing at an insect. Soon another fish does the same, and then another. Within minutes scores of similar images now punctuate the shimmering water, golden with the sun's retreating glow. Five feet in front of me a hefty trout, easily three pounds, explodes out of water like a porpoise. Now, well over a hundred fish, in a slashing, feeding frenzy, make the surface boil, devouring what I think are emerging caddis pupae. Or is the food of choice tonight tiny midges, hundreds of which cling to my waders? It makes a difference.

I cast repeatedly, intent upon hooking one of these robust Sacramento River rainbows. As they ignore my offerings I wonder in frustration, what *are* they eating? And even if I solve that puzzle, how do I cause a trout to take my singular offering among its hundreds, maybe thousands, of choices?

My concentration is broken when a flotilla of river otters swims toward me, looking more like corpulent reptiles than mammals. They disappear underwater and then surface again fifty feet in front of me. I count seven heads bobbing on the water, like beach balls, each one looking at me, as if inquiring, *what are you doing there?* And then, as though commanded, they all dive simultaneously and don't resurface until farther downriver.

With scorching temperatures elsewhere, it is at least fifteen degrees cooler here at river level and even more so when wading in the cold water, a refreshing respite from the stifling heat. The clean, churning water, infused with life-sustaining algae and insects, smells refreshingly crisp, like forest air heightened by a pungent aquatic aroma. It doesn't always smell this good, as when the river level is down and salmon carcasses accumulate and decay. Then the odor is one of death, but it's also a harbinger of life. But that's another story.

A flock of Canada geese suddenly appears from downriver, honking raucously as they fly past me in perfect V formation toward the setting sun. While savoring this sensual feast, I am abruptly jolted from my reflections when a strong heavy fish tears into the fly I left on the water. It rips line from my reel as it streaks away in a mad dash for freedom. For the next few minutes this power-packed dynamo runs, jumps, and tugs at the end of my line, determined not to come to my net.

I am immersed in a fly fisher's paradise.

It is a paradise I share with many others. Nearby are a white egret, always solitary it seems, and a great blue heron. I don't see the heron at first; instead, its eerie, piercing screech shatters the air, shocking me out of my reverie and sending shivers down my spine. I observe this bird in lumbering flight, its elongated body and extremities giving it a strange, almost prehistoric look.

A couple of times when standing in the water casting my fly, my senses have been rocked by a tumultuous crack a few feet from where I wade, almost like a lightning bolt striking right

next to me. After recovering my equilibrium, I see that a beaver is responsible. Swimming near the shore, it, too, must have been shocked to encounter this strange and perhaps threatening creature standing in the water. I can state unequivocally that few noises in the world of rivers are as jolting as a beaver's slap of its tail on the water's surface five feet away.

Although not as electrifying as a tail slap, having a large creature appear out of nowhere in the darkening evening, swimming toward me, is instantaneously terrifying. And then I see it is again a beaver, in this case a young one. Its mouth holds a batch of willow branches. For what purpose? Is it attempting to build a dam with these? Or eat them? I conclude it is a beaver doing what beavers do.

A beaver. Native to the Sacramento Valley, they were once numerous along the Sacramento River and Delta. David Schumacher.

Prologue

Ever since my wife and I moved to a home alongside the Sacramento River, we have been treated to many memorable scenes. It's always thrilling to see a salmon burst from the water. When I'm at river level casting for trout and this happens, usually I am at first startled by a large fish abruptly disrupting the prevailing mood. But then I feel comforted in knowing that yes, salmon do indeed occupy these waters. Sometimes it's a single jump. Other times the salmon explodes out of the water again and again and again, as though attempting to rid itself of demons. In fact, these are the last manifestations of the fish's tremendous stores of energy.

Myriad waterfowl scurry about the river's currents, take wing in its airways, and hunt in the water's depths and shallows. A personal favorite of mine is the common merganser, which I often see jetting up- or downriver inches above the water, anxious to get to its destination. In contrast, the cormorant, when not diving underwater for extended swims in pursuit of its prey, seems content to strike a regal pose on a rock or snag and rest for interminably long intervals.

Another choice companion is the belted kingfisher, distinctively handsome with its grayish blue, white, and black coloration and

Osprey with its catch of the day. Egon Harrasser.

Cormorants, voracious consumers of small fish. Bob Madgic.

disproportionately large beak and head with bushy crest. Always making its presence known, it chatters vociferously when it flies to a different tree branch, as though complaining about something. This beguiling bird definitely exhibits an attitude.

The top co-fisher is the osprey. It hovers high above water, staying in place for many long seconds, and then in what looks like a suicide dive, talons extended, collides with the water in a tumultuous crash. With admiration I quietly applaud the osprey when it emerges with one of those beautiful trout I too cherish. But unlike me, this legendary angler does not practice catch and release. Instead, once it works its way back out of the water to get airborne again, it rearranges the trout in its talons so as to be parallel with its own body for aerodynamic efficiency, and flies back to its nest to feed hungry mouths.

Deer on a morning visit to the river. Bob Madgic.

Once, I witnessed an osprey execute its dive, then struggle to leave the water. It couldn't and was carried downriver, all the while slapping its wings to get airborne again. Was the fish it caught too large a load? Was it injured? I couldn't decipher its predicament, and it eventually disappeared from sight.

Not all river companions are interested in water and fish. At times hundreds of swallows fill the air in pursuit of insects, these captivating birds swiftly and randomly darting, diving, and swooping in an unchoreographed ballet. A writing associate says that "watching swallows is one of the few things that will make me pause full minutes while fishing." This is true for me as well.

Presenting a sharp contrast in flying style are omnipresent turkey vultures. Unlike the tightly controlled movements of frenetic swallows, these expert gliders ride the air thermals, happy to go with the flow, even when winds are gale force. Then powerful air currents sweep them up, down, and across in broad creative strokes. When not soaring in the sky or keeping the land and river clean by stripping carcasses of flesh, vultures will often alight on a tree or fence posts and spread their wings to rest or dry.

And then there is the mysterious pull of the other side. Once the flapping wings of wild turkeys startled my boating companion and me when they suddenly flew close to our heads, intent on a river crossing. We often see deer swimming across this fast-moving river. It appears a perilous journey; sometimes the swimmer gets swept down a rocky rapid. I wonder: is the deer shunning something on the side it is leaving? Is an attraction on the opposite bank pulling it there? Or is change alone sufficient motivation to seek the other shore?

I once observed an unforgettable transaction between two of the river's grandest birds. As a golden eagle came downriver, its huge wings flapping as though in slow motion, an osprey, itself one of the larger birds, flew closely above the much bigger eagle. It kept swooping down and hitting the eagle's topside, like a black bird does to a hawk, confident that its flying agility will keep it safe. After disappearing downriver, the pair reappeared, now heading upriver, the osprey carrying out its same harassing antics. And then, remarkably, the eagle executed a 360-degree rotational turn in a desperate up-side-down maneuver to grab the osprey with its claws. It didn't succeed, and the birds eventually parted ways, the osprey having made its case for defending its territory.

Another time I witnessed dozens of Canada geese perform their standardized crash-landing technique, all screeching to a splashing halt directly in front of a lone egret motionlessly stalking its prey in shallow water. Despite this chaotic interruption to its disciplined agenda, the stoic egret never altered its statue-like pose. It *had* to have some instinctive reaction to the unexpected commotion right before its face, but if it did, it never betrayed what it was.

One memorable image was that of a bobcat hastily striding on top of the river bank below

A great white egret with a snack. Peter Park.

our home, not running but clearly serious about getting wherever it was going. In its mouth was a large feathery mass of white. Mission accomplished: egret for dinner tonight.

More images are recorded. Three hawks high in the sky engaged in what struck me as strange behavior. Two seemed to launch into a fight. They locked talons, and like a spiraling feather falling from the sky, the entangled pair spun ever downward, finally hitting the ground with a thud. Seemingly more surprised than hurt, the now identifiable redtail hawks disengaged, gathered their composure, and flew off, the battle apparently ending in a tie. Or so I thought. I later learned this episode was probably not one of enmity but rather one of romance and seduction.

The river and shorelines are always changing. When we first moved here, a large section of land upriver extended out from the shoreline. And then at flood stage, the rampaging river plowed through this peninsula and created a small island. This picturesque feature, still richly vegetated with trees and bushes, stayed in place for a few years, until raging waters tested its durability. By the time the water subsided, only a few willow bushes clung to what little ground remained. These, too, disappeared when the next high flows stripped their roots free. All that's left today of the original land form is a small resistant remnant still jutting out from shore like the elbow of a slightly bent arm. As the river's flow meets it, the current is pushed outward to form a graceful arc. This remnant, too, will surely erode away to create a new pattern of land and water.

River currents. Bob Madgic.

"Redtail Hawk." Many species of raptor birds are prevalent along the river. Bob Madgic.

Low water brings surprises. At very low levels, a rocky section emerges in the river's middle. It becomes a focal point for life, especially when salmon carcasses get stranded there. One of my wife's favorite scenes was that of a golden eagle and a bald eagle occupying the same rock, seemingly sharing a salmon carcass. We have seen a family of otters doing the same, and as many as five bald eagles on the rocks consuming fish remains. Often vultures will stand nearby, ready to clean up what remains. And gulls, too, will flutter about, alight here and there, to add to the aviary spectacle. Greenery soon coats the rocky outcroppings when they are exposed to air. A cluster of yellow flowers once sprouted, providing a floral centerpiece to this sumptuous river-buffet setting.

The rocky section is part of a long ledge that runs across the channel, out from where our home sits on the bluff. It creates a considerable rapid, always emitting river music that varies across the year with changing river levels. The water crashes and churns constantly, the thrashing tempo blotting out all other sounds. Open our bedroom slider, and the river speaks to us all night long, passing on its many messages.

The river indeed blesses all those who come to occupy her realm.

The Sacramento River in the Bend area exemplifies the natural river. Bob Madgic.

CHAPTER ONE

A Natural River

"Let the waters bring forth abundantly the moving creature that hath life, and fowl that may fly above the earth in the open firmament of heaven."

—*Genesis 1:20*

AT ONE TIME, THE SACRAMENTO VALLEY represented nature at her grandest. Behind its lush creation and sustenance was a river.

The river had many origins. Mt. Shasta's vast snowpack fed a massive underground reservoir of aquifers and springs. Water bubbled out of rock crevices and inaugurated tiny rivulets that made meadows bloom and sing. In the nearby Mt. Eddy mountain range, newly formed streams gushed down slopes. All these waters gathered as a single powerful river, then roared through a narrow gorge.

As the river plummeted within a granite and forested ravine, other waterways joined, adding volume and force. Torrents fed by snow and rain eroded hillsides; dislodged stones and boulders formed rock gardens as the river rushed onward.

Emerging from the canyon, the river was shadowed by mountains on either side. They collected massive quantities of snow, its melt destined for the river. Farther down the valley, two large tributaries delivered yet more water, this time from the Sierra Nevada.

The river grew in size, and its gradient flattened, its current slowed. Its load was reduced to smaller and smaller gravel, until only fine sediment and decomposed plant matter remained. Wherever it settled, the sediment provided substance and nutrition to river life.

From its very beginnings, the river sought to bend and turn, the way of all waterways. Tiny streams that form from melting glaciers will meander even when there are no obstructions, as do ocean currents. The river that follows a straight course is rare, unless constricted by something like rock walls.

Now free to wander, the broadening river soon twisted like a large slithering serpent, creating a complex mosaic of wide looping bends, deep pools, shallow riffles, back eddies, and oxbows. Its ever-shifting currents sculpted sandbars and carved out banks. Land rises stood as high as ten to fifteen feet and several miles wide in places.

Profuse rain and snow caused water to accumulate and then rage. Torrential flows scoured the river's bed, flushed out debris, moved gravel and sediment. Surges of water overflowed the channel, flooding outlying lands. This flood plain spread over a million acres and regularly extended thirty miles beyond the channel.

One of three forks of the Sacramento River in the Mt. Eddy watershed, major providers of water for the river. Bob Madgic.

Composed mainly of silt and clay, the sponge-like land stored huge quantities of water that slowly seeped into the ground or retreated back to the river. Pollutants were filtered out, the water cleansed. As the water receded, it left gravel and sand bars. Such ebbs and flows allowed some creatures to spawn and grow, and plants to regenerate.

The volume of water entering the valley filled every cavity, depression, lowland, and channel. The entire region was replete with wetlands. Integrated among them were millions of acres of bulrushes, or tules, and other aquatic plants.

Periodic mass flooding would create a gigantic inland sea that extended more than 100 miles from the foothills to the coastal ranges, forming one of America's largest freshwater wetlands. Rather than damaging and destroying life, such flooding created and sustained it.

Lush riparian habitat was everywhere: high canopies of cottonwood, sycamore, walnut, ash, and oak trees; dense masses of willow shrubs, grapevines, and hanging lianas; thick carpets of fruit-laden bushes, grasses, and herbs. The copious transpiration, succulent leaves, and rapid generation of trees and shrubs created a shady,

Old growth riparian forests as seen here are rare along today's river. Bob Madgic.

cool and moist microclimate, a virtual greenhouse environment.

These riverside jungles kept floods in check. Roots secured the banks, preventing excessive silt from entering the river and smothering fish-spawning gravel. When extreme flooding caused banks to crumble and large quantities of clay to enter the waterway, the river cleansed itself merely by flowing. Meanwhile, new banks formed elsewhere to replace those lost, as the river always sought to achieve equilibrium.

Beyond the riparian forests—generally defined as those that regularly flooded—were millions of acres of woodlands and meadows. Dominating the landscape were gigantic and stately valley oaks, the largest of all oak tree species and unique to California.

The river and its multifaceted surroundings nurtured and sustained one of the most prolific arrays of mammals, birds, amphibians, and fishes in the world. Countless elk, black and grizzly bears, mule deer, and pronghorn ante-

Tule elk, an iconic California mammal, now live mainly in preserves. Bob Madgic.

Bobcats are vital for controlling rodent populations. Trish Carney.

The native western pond turtle.
U.S. Fish and Wildlife Service.

Vernal pools form from winter rains, with perimeter wildflowers blooming as the water retreats. Bob Madgic.

Tundra swans were once numerous in the Sacramento Valley wetlands. Mike Peters.

lope roamed the valley, resembling scenes from the African Serengeti and Great American Prairie. More than five hundred thousand tule elk, another California original, grazed valley lands. As many as ten thousand grizzly bears occupied California—the most in any state and roughly twenty percent of the entire North American population.

A multitude of aquatic species, amphibians and reptiles—including the giant garter snake that reached five feet in length—lived in the swamps and marshes. Every spring, rainwater gathered in depressions across the varied terrains and formed countless vernal pools, giving life to a surprising diversity of organisms that emerged from dormancy to enjoy resurgent life, like the fairy shrimp and spadefoot toads.

Few river corridors attracted as many resident and migrating birds—more than 250 species. Millions of birds, some from as far away as the Arctic, descended to this valley, including the abundant honking Canada geese, exquisitely beautiful greater sandhill cranes and tundra swans, and striking snow geese, magnificent in their profuse whiteness.

The forests and woodlands—home to species like the yellow-billed magpie, tri-colored blackbird, Nuttall's woodpecker, and the least bell's vireo—also attracted resplendent neotropical migratory birds. Bank and cliff swallows darted and swirled, swooping over water and fields, catching insects on the wing. Numerous eagles, hawks, falcons, harriers, and other raptor species soared everywhere, feasting on waterfowl, rodents, small birds—and, in the case of osprey, fish.

Runs of spring run Chinook salmon now occur mainly in Butte Creek, both shown here. Scott McReynolds.

The river itself held an unparalleled assemblage of cold- and warm-water fishes. The main waterway and its arteries that probed deep into the Cascade and Sierra Nevada mountain ranges gave rise to more trout species than found anywhere in the world. In the river's lower stretches lived the oldest and largest freshwater fishes in the world—white sturgeon and its smaller cousin, the green sturgeon.

The linchpin of the entire river community was salmon. At one time, millions left the Pacific Ocean annually and entered the bay's narrow opening (the Golden Gate) to return to their galaxy of freshwater birthplaces. There they delivered vital ocean nutrients that nourished flora and fauna throughout the watershed.

The McCloud River redband trout is one of California's prettiest and rarest native trout. California Department of Fish and Game.

While nurturing life all along its extensive route, the river still had much more to do near its end. As its current faded and the marshes expanded, another large river flowed in from the south. These combined waters, carrying only the finest of sediment, blended in a massive labyrinth encompassing thousands of braided

Surrounding the estuary were untold acres of marshes and wetlands, and hundreds of miles of tule swamps, ponds, mudflats, and seasonally inundated islands of dense forests. The soil was composed of organically rich silt and layers of peat, fifty feet deep in places.

This complex and intricate milieu supported

River otters are widespread throughout the Sacramento River. Brian Kreb.

channels and islands. Water and silt converged and exited the valley through a tight opening, rather than diverging, as happens with most rivers. In the process an inverted delta was formed, one of the few in the world.

Saltwater from the Pacific Ocean regularly surged into the freshwater mass. The combined currents of this estuary circulated in a choreographed pattern, enriched by what the rivers brought from distant mountains and foothills, and what incoming tides brought from the sea.

one of the world's richest webs of life, from microscopic phytoplankton and zooplankton to the largest mammals, from tiny minnows to giant sturgeon.

Most of the water that entered the estuary eventually drained to the Pacific Ocean after passing through an elaborate system of bays and straits, then squeezing through the constricted mouth of the bay. During floods, when rivers thundered into the estuary, the outflows pushed far out in the ocean. Residual sediment

Mallard duck. Mike Peters.

from distant mountains bolstered beaches that many organisms relied on for propagation and sustenance.

The river thus connected the mountains with the sea and was the conduit for salmon and other anadromous species to bring the sea's nutrients to the mountains. But the ocean was not an ending. As water evaporated from its surface, it would return as precipitation to Mt. Shasta, Mt. Eddy, and the surrounding Cascade and Sierra Nevada ranges. There, it would recharge the river's beginnings, and the unceasing cycle of life would continue.

Sacramento Valley wildlife refuges provide critical sanctuaries for migrating and resident waterfowl.
Mike Peters.

Lower Falls, McCloud River. Bob Madgic.

CHAPTER TWO

River as Community

"The first peace, which is the most important, is that which comes within the souls of people when they realize their relationship, their oneness, with the universe and all its powers, and when they realized that at the center of the universe dwells the Great Spirit, and this center is really everywhere, it is within each of us."

—Black Elk

ARTIFACTS REVEAL THAT SMALL ISOLATED groups of humans entered Northern California thousands of years ago. These were highly mobile family clusters that hunted and gathered primarily in upland country.

A larger, more cohesive population appeared in Northern California about six thousand years ago. Linguistic studies, along with archeological findings of village structures and artifacts such as bow and arrow weaponry, bone fishhooks and pendants, show that such a faction—the Wintun family—came down from the north. One grouping settled in the northern valley. From there they spread out, following the salmon-laden waters of the Upper Sacramento, McCloud, and Trinity rivers, as well as other smaller waterways. Over time they divided into nine bands or tribelets, each socially independent and with a well-defined territory.

Other tribes established villages and dwellings on or near the Sacramento River south of the Wintu territories. These included the Nomlaki people. Their territory began at Cottonwood Creek and extended to Thomes Creek.

Another contingent—the Patwin—continued southward and became one of the largest Indian nations in California. Their lands were located primarily on the western side of the river, from the mid-valley region to the river's estuary. This largely inhospitable area experienced rampant flooding, which created vast wetlands and sloughs, tule-choked marshes, boggy islands, and vine-strewn jungles encompassing huge cottonwoods, sycamores, ashes, and oaks.

Inhabiting lands east of the river to the foothills were the Maidu and Nisenan tribes. Though farther from the river than other tribes, they still were nourished by it.

These native peoples believed that they, the rivers, forests, rocks, and all creatures were connected parts of Mother Earth—an integrated, self-sustaining community. With minimal adjustments they accepted the world wherein they lived and adapted to its rhythms. Resisting the forces of nature or trying to contain them was not their way.

Above all, these were river people.

The Wintu

Upper canyon waterways combined to form the large river the Wintu called *Num-tee-pom-all-way-nem,* or *Ol-te-ma* (today's Sacramento River). The tribe located its central villages below this confluence. The mountains, meadows, woodlands, and especially the river provided the Wintu with all the food they needed. They ate deer, elk, pronghorn, bear, and other small mammals typically killed with bows and arrows. They consumed sugar and grey pine nuts, "fruit balls" from the buckeye tree, dried grasshoppers, berries, grasses, seeds, grapes, wild onions, potatoes, and cabbage, along with other plants and roots.

One of their most important foods fell from the region's abundant oak trees—acorns. Seven varieties of oaks grew in Northern California: valley, black, blue, live, Oregon, oracle, and scrub. One of nature's densest foods, an acorn has high fat, carbohydrate, and protein content. An adult Wintu probably consumed up to two thousand pounds of acorns each year.

A Wintu chief as he prepares to hunt game. Livingston Stone Collection.

Wintu arrow and spear heads, fishing weight, mortar, and pestle. Bob Madgic.

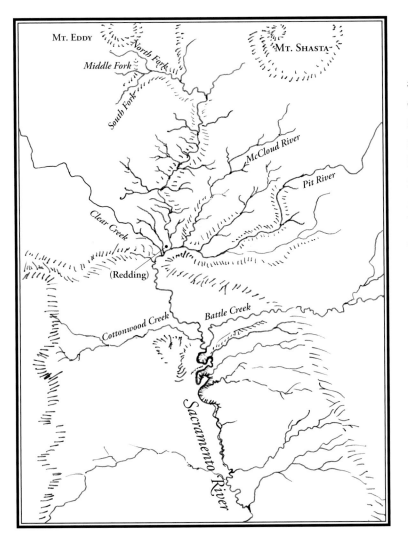

The upper and middle Sacramento River before the arrival of Euro-Americans. Walt Simmons and Marti Weidert.

The Wintu's primary food source was fish. The river and its tributaries held salmon, sea-run rainbow trout, resident or non-migrating rainbow trout, Sacramento sucker, pikeminnow, and hardhead. The Wintu consumed them all. They also ate shellfish, once abundant in the rivers and streams of Northern California. These included the pearl mussel, Western ridge mussel, and the scalloped juga, a small snail. (Such shellfish species, which helped to keep waters pure, have since disappeared from the region's waterways mainly due to pollution.)

No fish contributed as much to the Wintu diet and culture as salmon. To catch them, the Wintu built fishing stations. They extended a large log from shore to two crossed stakes secured in the river bottom. A spear-wielding fisherman then stood on the log to watch for salmon passing below. Another technique involved "salmon houses." The Wintu would drive two large crossed stakes into the river bottom, then lash horizontal poles that extended from the stakes to the shore to create a frame. They built a wicker hut on the frame with holes in the floor for salmon viewing and spearing. To see the salmon better they sometimes covered the river bottom below their perch with white rocks.

For spears the Wintu used ten- to twenty-foot-long harpoons. These had two wooden prongs about six to eight inches long, each with a sharply pointed thimble made of a special hardwood or deer bone. When a salmon was speared, two toggles affixed to the ends of the prongs came loose and pivoted at right angles, which kept the barbs from withdrawing. Attached to the shaft was a cord made of buckskin or woven fibers, which prevented the fish from swimming off with the harpoon.

Still another fishing method employed weirs—structures or pens that entrapped fish. The Wintu constructed one type of weir by driving wooden posts into the river bottom so close together that fish could not pass through. They used rocks for another—closing off the entrance when fish swam into the weir. They could then easily catch their prey with either nets or spears.

The people also used lines and hooks. For

line they wove threads from the leaves of wild iris plants or twisted strands from the bark of milkweed or dogbane plants. They made hooks from deer jawbone or from a fish. They fished below salmon spawning beds, where steelhead, trout, and other species gorged on dislodged salmon roe. The fisherman sometimes baited his hook with dried roe that dispersed its juices when impaled on the hook.

The tribe's many methods of preparing and preserving salmon gave them year-round fare. Fresh fish were roasted on flat rocks or cedar planks heated over a fire. To create an oven-like effect, they covered the fish with large saxifrage leaves and placed hot ashes on the leaves. They either ate the roasted salmon or pulverized it into fine meal—salmon flour. To preserve the flour, they added salt. Nuts or dried salmon eggs—considered a delicacy—added extra flavor. The Wintu also preserved fish through drying. They would impale several splayed-out, fresh carcasses on a long pole, then place the pole in the sun or over a fire.

To ensure a sustainable harvest of salmon, the Wintu developed a system of territorial rights among the varied bands and villages. Each group only took fish from its river or section of river. With so many salmon, disputes were rare.

The Winnemem Wintu

Nowhere was the attachment to water deeper and more enduring than with a band of Wintu who built their villages on the banks of the McCloud River. This icy cold waterway could be traced to the meadow spring from where these people believed they originated.

Buliyum Puiyuk (Mt. Shasta) was the center of their world. It was where the great Creator, *Olelbes*, resided, and where their souls returned after death—first up the flower trail to Mt. Shasta and then on to the Milky Way. And with

their birthplace being the sacred spring, water would always guide their spiritual beliefs and way of life.

The McCloud was the middle river among three major ones in the region (Upper Sacramento, McCloud, Pit), so these people called it *We-nem-mem* (*mem* means water in their language), meaning "middle waters." They were the "middle river" people—the Winnemem Wintu.

The Winnemem were dependent upon and devoted to salmon. Each year they welcomed these revered creatures back to the McCloud River, one of the most productive salmon waterways in the world due to its frigid waters. It supported three runs of salmon: spring, fall, and winter. The most and biggest fish came with the spring run, averaging twenty pounds. Some specimens weighed as much as seventy pounds.

The salmon halted their journey below the McCloud's lower falls, which the Winnemem called *Nurum-wit-ti-dekkit*, or "falls where the salmon turn back." There the people built a village called *Nur-um-witipon* ("salmon come back"). The men lashed stout poles to form catwalks over the water, enabling them to spear passing fish. Reportedly, six men speared more than five hundred salmon in one evening, averaging five hundred pounds per man. Only Wintu men speared and harvested this mighty fish. The youth developed their skills on the smaller, more lethargic suckers.

One of the most sacred places on the McCloud River was near a rock shaped like a salmon's heart in the river's lower reaches. Lines in this rock resembled arteries; the black earth nearby resembled blood vessels along the salmon's backbone. The Winnemem came often to "salmon heart rock" to catch these treasured fish.

To honor salmon, the Winnemem swam below waterfalls along the river each year, as

Panther Meadows on the slopes of Mt. Shasta, near where the Wintu's sacred spring is located. Bob Madgic.

Middle Falls, McCloud River. Bob Madgic.

salmon did. They believed their fate was linked to the salmon's. If the salmon disappeared, the people would as well.

In the Winnemem's world, every natural element was related and vitally important. Each depended on the others, whether the sucker, salmon, chipmunk, deer, wren, eagle, worm, frog, mushroom, acorn, fallen leaf, tree, insect, or stone.

They believed the great Creator, Olelbes, wanted them to care for Mother Earth. When necessary they used fire to rid the forests of brush; they knew that an unkempt forest was unhealthy and that some plants require fire to germinate. They gathered acorns for consumption and to keep the forests from becoming overgrown.

All water was sacred to the Winnemem Wintu: streams, rivers, springs, vernal pools, even standing ponds. All possessed healing powers—for treating wounds and physical ailments, for cleansing and purifying the body, for bolstering the spirit. The people prayed to these waters and looked to them for guidance. But the McCloud River gave them their identity. It imparted knowledge and taught them; it sustained them and kept them healthy. The river needed the people as much as they needed it. They would ensure that it always flowed freely and be kept from impurities. In protecting it they believed they were playing their role alongside the raccoon, stonefly, sucker fish, mollusk, and other organisms that also did this work. It was their life's mission.

They reveled in the river's presence. The simple act of drinking water became a rapturous experience as they plunged into the river, spraying water high in the air. To gather clams, a Winnemem would dive to the bottom, linger amphibian-like, and then emerge with a clam in each hand and mouth.

Tribe members submerged in the river to bathe their bodies and purify their souls. On a spiritual quest a man might first go to the mountains and fast for many days. Upon returning he would chant and meditate in an earthen lodge filled with smoke to rid his body of impurities. Afterward the man would go to the river and swim. He emerged from the water cleansed and stronger.

Other times a man might leave the village to seek an isolated spot alongside the river. He entered the water naked and swam along the bottom. Leaving the river's currents, he prayed on its banks. He fasted. He slept. He recounted his dreams. Physically weakened, he might experience visions. Upon completing this river quest he returned to the village mentally refurbished.

Women, too, used the river for cleansing and transformation. According to Wintu practices (and those of most other Native American tribes), a menstruating woman was shunned from village life. She stayed alone in a cedar house, consuming only soup. Her unclean state was seen as one of defilement, even injury, and presumed to affect those connected to her. So her husband would also avoid activities like hunting, because he, too, was weakened and subject to bad luck. When a female's cycle ended she would cleanse and purify her body by swimming in the river.

Certain river pools, rocks and rock formations, caves, and other natural phenomena held special meaning to the Winnemem. They believed spiritual beings and other powers resided there. For instance, a male could enhance his hunting and fishing prowess if he swam in a particular pool. Rubbing the polished knob on a special rock in the McCloud River would heighten his powers of fertility. Another smooth, rounded rock—called the "blessing rock"—symbolized the circle of life. The people would run their hand all around this stone, seeking a blessing from the rock in exchange for their caresses.

Adults would bring their young to "children's rock." They believed it would magnify a child's special gifts and propensity toward goodness.

"Puberty rock" symbolized a female's transition to adulthood. The Winnemem held a four-day puberty ceremony near this rock that corresponded with lunar and seasonal cycles. The young woman camped along the river for three nights. There older women imparted knowledge and taught her skills, like how to grind herbs into medicines. On the fourth day, when the moon was full, she swam across the river, now a full-fledged woman. The tribe celebrated her transition to adulthood with a coming-of-age ceremony and feast. (This ceremony continues to this day.)

The Winnemem buried their dead near the river so the spirits of the deceased would remain close to it. These burial sites, too, became sacred. All of these connections to the river nourished the tribe and kept it balanced with Mother Earth. They worked in harmony with all life forms to care for her.

To honor their birthplace and the river's, the Winnemem Wintu returned each year to the sacred spring on the slope of Mt. Shasta. There they prayed for help in caring for the earth, thanked the spring for its gifts and pledged to always carry out their mission. In return they asked the sacred spring to keep the people and their river healthy. As a chieftain stated, "We came out of the water so we return back to it. In our doing so, we make the water happy, and happy water flows better across the earth, including that in our own river."

The Nomlaki

Nomlaki territory began where Cottonwood Creek entered the waterway. The River Nomlaki resided along the river; Hill Nomlaki lived from the foothills to the crest of the high coastal range.

The River Nomlaki occupied a small area. The southernmost extremity was near Thomes Creek, barely forty miles south of Cottonwood Creek. Like many Indians in the region, they escaped the searing summer heat by moving temporarily to the mountains.

Salmon provided the River Nomlaki with more food than they could consume. They traded fish with hill people for meat, seeds, and acorns. In a well-coordinated system, the tribes shared their respective bounties, although conflict occurred between the two groups as well.

The Nomlaki were good hunters—unique from other river tribes in that they actively hunted grizzly bear. Only the highly skilled undertook this dangerous feat. Substantial quantities of meat and a warm, tradeable pelt proved an enticing reward.

The Nomlaki population totaled about two thousand before contacts with white men decimated them.

The Patwin

Legend of the Flood. Of old the Indians abode tranquilly in the Sacramento Valley and were happy. All on a sudden there was a might and swift rushing of waters, so that the whole valley became like the Big Water, which no man can measure. The Indians fled for their lives, but a great many were overtaken by the waters, and they slept beneath the waves.

⁓

Downriver from the Nomlaki on the river's western side were the Patwin territories. Like

Tules, shown here, once covered thousands of acres of Delta wetlands. Walt Simmons.

the Nomlaki, these people divided into river and hill tribes, such as the Suisun (on the bay since named for them); the Napa, who lived in a beautiful valley (also named after them); and the Korusi (whose name has been altered to Colusa).

The lands of river-oriented tribes included immense wetlands and plains. Winter floods created swamps and brought swarms of gnats and mosquitoes. Few trees meant little wood. So the Patwin located their major villages on smaller waterways, such as Putah Creek, Stony Creek, Cache Creek, and Napa River. Yet, because they depended on the river for their main sustenance, they constructed temporary shelters or camps on whatever solid ground existed in the wetlands when they hunted and fished.

They also built dwellings on the huge flood plain, usually on bluffs. Sometimes they assembled mounds upon which to place their homes. A house commonly was a dome-like structure, with walls made of tules, reeds, and mud for added warmth. Reedy substrate carpeted the floors for bedding and insulation. The doorway was often placed at the top of these structures, accessed with lashed-pole ladders. It also served as a chimney. Summer huts were taller, more flimsy structures with a frame of lashed switches covered with tules.

These homes were not built to last, and for good reason. Winter storms and spring run-off often brought massive flooding, sometimes creating a vast inland sea. When this happened the Indians sought safety elsewhere. After the floods receded, they returned to their former sites and simply built anew. They expected such occurrences as part of Mother Earth's cycles.

Throughout the lower river, water temper-

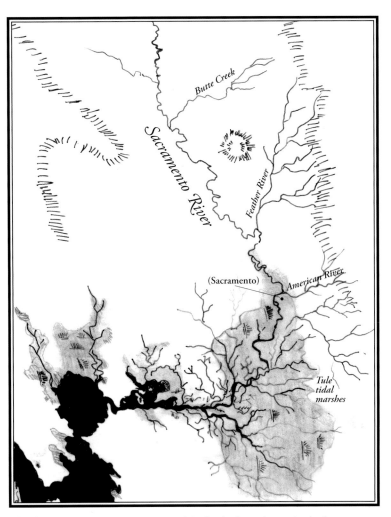

The lower Sacramento River and Delta before the arrival of Euro-Americans. Walt Simmons and Marti Weidert.

atures were much warmer than in its upper reaches. This meant a wider variety of fish. Though salmon was the choice catch, Patwin fished for the ancient sturgeon, perch, chub, sucker, pikeminnow, and migrating steelhead. Turtles were also a staple, roasted directly over a fire.

Like the Wintu, the Patwin used a catwalk system and salmon houses to spear fish from above their swimming routes. The waterway's enormous breadth here required watercraft. The Indians carved boats from cottonwood or sycamore logs. They also lashed together bundles of tules to create buoyant—albeit clumsy—tule canoes. To propel these crafts they used either long willow poles to push off the bottom, or paddles made from oak branches. Such

The Patwin people used tules for many purposes, including summer dwellings. Walt Simmons.

canoe-like boats enabled them to navigate networks of reedy wetlands to fish and hunt for waterfowl, as well as to spear passing fish.

The Patwin were masters of net and ensnarement techniques. They usually placed large nets made from willow poles and vine or thatched-grass webbings into a restricted area, or "pen," out in the river, and then directed salmon, giant sturgeon, and other species into the nets. They used smaller nets or spears to harvest the cloistered fish. The nets also came in handy for capturing fowl, like mud hens, quail, geese, and ducks.

Similar to the Wintu, the Patwin allocat-ed fishing rights to each village for a specific section of river. An outsider wishing to fish a section had to gain permission from the village chieftain.

Beyond the marshlands and plains were vast riparian forests of oaks, cottonwoods, and sycamores. The oaks provided the Patwin with acorns. Through a communal system similar to that for fishing, village chiefs assigned collection rights for this prized food in specific areas to certain groups.

The tribes consumed cattails, tule roots, wild garlic, and potatoes, among numerous other plants. Women baked, dried, or steamed plant roots. They used mortars to grind plants into flour for cakes.

Women all along the Sacramento River excelled in basket weaving, using the abundant reeds that grew near the water. They made utilitarian baskets for gathering and storage and highly artistic ones for trading.

The Maidu

Native Americans gravitated to the confluences of today's Sacramento and Feather rivers, and Sacramento and American rivers. By the early 1800s, approximately ten thousand native people occupied villages there. These were the Maidu people; a sub-branch was the Maidu-Nisenan, or just Nisenan. Many of them lived in an area on the American River they called Natomas, meaning "north place" or "upstream people."

These tribes typically established their villages on high ground. They covered their dome-shaped dwellings with bark or brush and often placed them over slight depressions for added coolness in hot weather. In contrast to the bleak Patwin territory, this side of the river was lush with vegetation. The waters teemed with salmon, steelhead, trout, perch, ducks, geese, turtles, crawdads, mussels, clams, and bullfrogs. Grasslands and forests supported elk, pronghorn antelope, bear, deer, rabbits, doves, quail, and many other animal and bird species, along with a myriad of plants. To support their evolving society, the industrious Maidu built granaries, milling equipment, and a host of weapons and tools. They used many of these in trade with other tribes.

Maidu lived intermittently in a prominent refuge on the eastern side of the river—a small range of volcanic remnants jutting up from the plains. This circular mountain cluster (today's Sutter Buttes) encompassed seventy-five square miles, with a diameter of only ten miles. The highest peak, South Butte, stood more than two thousand feet above sea level. Two hundred to three hundred feet lower were North Butte and West Butte, respectively. During massive floods Maidu people fled there and waited for the water to recede. Artifacts and grinding holes in rocks show that tribes also occupied these highlands during the brutally hot summers.

The Maidu called the Buttes "*Histum Yani*," meaning "Middle Mountains of the Valley" or "Spirit Mountain." According to legend, the first people were created there, and after death, their spirits rested in the Buttes before the journey to the afterlife.

~

Native Americans who settled in the Sacramento River Valley, either along the main river or on smaller waterways, were blessed with moderate weather, forests, valleys, wetlands, and large populations of mammals, birds, and fish. Inevitable conflicts arose with other tribes living in more marginal regions. The Wintu, for instance, fiercely defended their lands from the Yana people to the east and the Shasta people to the north. Nonetheless, history shows Sacramento Valley tribes lived as peacefully as any in North America. Their tribal rights systems for fishing and acorn collection, and their widespread trade with other Indians, were surely exemplary among native peoples.

What sustained all these river people and made them less contentious was the bountiful river and its tributaries that flowed by their villages and provided them with salmon and other foods. They in turn treated this river, indeed all of nature, with respect and humility. It was an integrated community, each part co-existing with others so all could flourish.

Rice farms cover hundreds of square miles of the Sacramento Valley. Bruce King.

Chapter Three

River as Resource

> "By the mid-eighteenth century the invention of new technologies had begun whereby we could manipulate our environment to our own advantage. At this time also an 'objective world' was born—a world clearly distinct from ourselves and available not as a means of divine communion, but as a vast realm of natural resources for exploitation and consumption."
>
> —Thomas Berry

To the Native Americans living in the Sacramento Valley, humans, rivers, forests, lands, stones, and all creatures were tightly knitted together. Keeping this community intact and healthy was the river coursing alongside their villages and the supreme fish that provided them with sustenance—Chinook salmon.

Indians did manipulate their surroundings, including the river, however lightly. Their purpose was not domination, but survival. They constructed footbridges to cross rivers, scaffolds from which to spear fish, and weirs to trap them; they made mounds to elevate their dwellings above flood waters; they regularly burned lands. Whether such efforts would have become more disruptive as Indian populations grew is not known. But these native peoples attempted to live in concert with the natural world, not work against it. To resist natural forces such as flooding was not only futile, it ran counter to that which guided their lives—adapting to the world in which they lived.

The newcomers who arrived with American expansion viewed the natural world differently. They believed it first had to be subdued and then put to human purposes. Natural resources existed to be tapped and utilized, little more than commodities for generating income. Each wave of newcomers who came to the Sacramento Valley acted on such beliefs.

Exploration

The Sacramento River at first served as a conduit for travel, something to be followed and, if possible, navigated. It was a highway of many names, variously called the Piscadore, the Spanish River, the Jesús María, the River of Destruction, the Buenaventura (Good Fortune), the River of the North, and the name it bears today.

The Spanish conquistadors were the first to arrive in what they called New Spain. In 1808, Gabriel Moraga came searching for new mission sites so Spanish friars could convert native "savages" to Christianity. He also sought to find and punish recalcitrant Indians who had resisted earlier conversion efforts. After traveling up the Central Valley, Moraga and his soldiers camped along one of many rivers they discovered. Enthralled by the lush oak and cottonwood forest, trees laced with grapevines, crisp air filled with birdsong, and clear blue waters populated by countless fish, Moraga exclaimed, *"¡Es como el sagrado sacramento!"* ("This is like the holy sacrament!")

Moraga had described today's Feather River, which he subsequently named the Sacramento. Two days later he named the river joining it from the northwest (today's Sacramento River) the Jesús María. The combined river below the confluence retained the name Sacramento. Moraga proceeded north but soon stopped, later reporting that he found no likely places for another mission and too many Indians to subdue.

In 1817, Luís Antonio Arguello and Friar Narciso Duran followed in Moraga's footsteps.

The river that Moraga called the Sacramento, Arguello named El Río de las Plumas, or "River of Feathers," based on the huge number of waterfowl he saw. Later it was simplified to Feather River. The Spaniards then pushed up the Jesús María another one hundred miles, where the river flowed through rolling reddish hills (a feature that would later lead to the name Red Bluff). But, like Moraga, Arguello and Duran did not find any good mission sites and departed.

Russian explorers were also active in Northern California at this time. They probed south from Alaska to a place on the northern coast they called New Albion. In 1812, the Russians erected Fort Ross nearby, "Ross" being a likely phonetic truncation of *Rossiia*, or Russia.

In 1818, Russian explorer Ivan Kusov searched inland. His party entered San Francisco Bay by boat and then remarkably sailed a small ship

The river near Red Bluff. Tim Palmer.

"Jedediah Smith's Party Crossing the Burning Mohave Desert." Painting by Frederick Remington.

nearly seventy miles up the estuary's snaking waterways and vast wetlands. He ventured up a channel as far as today's American River—the first known boat journey on the Sacramento. The Russians left the region and never returned.

Spain lost control of New Spain in 1821 to Mexico, which named the territory Alta California. Among the region's earliest explorers were American trappers and mountain men, most notably Jedediah Smith.

In the fall of 1826, Smith and his party crossed Utah and arrived at Mission San Gabriel in Southern California. Smith, a devout Methodist, always carried a Bible and rifle. A prominent scar from a grizzly-bear encounter marked his face. The Mexican governor considered Smith and his men illegal immigrants and insisted they leave. Smith did as instructed, then angled northward over the Tehachapi Mountains and up the San Joaquin Valley, skirmishing with Indians along the way. In April of 1827, his party reached the confluence of the Sacramento and American rivers, where the Nisenan Indians greeted them peacefully. Smith only stayed a few days before returning to Utah by way of the Sierra Nevada.

Smith launched a second expedition to Alta California the next year. He followed the meandering river he knew as the Buenaventura (today's Sacramento). Far upriver he and his men and three hundred horses had to cross the water where steep bluffs impeded their travel. As he reported in his diary: "I moved on with the intention of traveling up the Buenaventura but soon found the rocky hills coming in so close to the river to make it impossible to travel. I went in advance of the party and ascending a high point took a view of the country and found the river coming [from] the NE and running apparently for 20 or 30 miles through ragged rocky hills. The mountain beyond appeared too high to cross at that season of the year or perhaps at any other."

Smith's party briefly camped downriver before crossing the coastal range and entering the vast redwood forests. (Located here today is Jedediah Smith State Park on the Smith River.) They continued north, eventually following the Willamette River to the Columbia River and on to Vancouver, Washington, home to the British-owned Hudson Bay Company. Smith told company officials of his discoveries and

Overlook at Iron Canyon, where Jedediah Smith scanned the river and concluded his party had to cross it in order to continue. Today it is called Jed's Overlook. Garry Bagula.

then headed back to the Southwest. He died in 1831 when he was killed by Indians near Taos, New Mexico.

The Hudson Bay Company, the largest fur-trading outpost on the West Coast, had earlier sent its trappers to California. Acting on Smith's information, it did so again in the early 1830s. Its men gathered furs for many months, then left the region. Their main legacy was the decimation of the native tribes, not by warfare but by diseases they unknowingly brought with them. Other trappers and explorers also passed them on to Indian guides or by other direct contacts. Lacking immunity, the natives were particularly vulnerable to diseases such as malaria and smallpox, which annihilated up to seventy-five percent of the Indians in the Central Valley. As reported by American trapper George Yount in his diary: "The bodies of un-told thousands lay withering on the plains and fertile valleys…deserted and desolated villages stood tenantless all over the valley."

Life along the river was forever changed and would continue to be altered with each new onslaught of Euro-Americans.

Settlers Arrive

Those who came after the trappers to the Sacramento Valley found—as had the native people—a hospitable place along a bountiful river. One of the first was a Swiss immigrant, Johann Augustus Sutter, his name later Americanized to John Sutter. In 1841, Sutter bought the remains of Fort Ross, which the Russians had abandoned, and moved much of the materials far up the Sacramento River. There, a few miles inland, he began construction on a fort. His workers, including many Nisenan, made bricks from the region's pervasive clay soil. Sutter named the completed sprawling garrison New Helvetia (New Switzerland), with many of his workers serving as its protectors.

A town took root. Shops were built beyond the fort; tents and flimsy wooden buildings sprouted closer to the river. Sutter himself planted two thousand fruit trees. Word of the settlement spread, particularly in Yerba Buena (San Francisco). At this time few in that port town had any interest in the wild inland region; indeed, most people feared it. But along the Pacific Coast the frontier no longer lay westward, but eastward, and this is where the adventuresome headed. Their main avenue was the Sacramento River.

What the first newcomers found in New Helvetia was a small encampment with mainly tents as living quarters. Squatters were everywhere. The stench of human excreta permeated the air, especially oppressive during stifling hot weather. Still, the river town offered promise, and it soon bustled with activity. Docks were built; more shipping and trading enterprises got underway.

To foster business development, Sutter's son, John August Sutter Jr., joined with Sam Brannan, a recent transplant from Maine. Arriving in New Helvetia in 1847, Brannan had started a supply business, and then a newspaper, the *California Star,* which later became the *Daily Alta California.* Both Sutter Jr. and Brannan believed this new outpost should be called "Sacramento." The elder Sutter wanted "Sutter" in the name, but Sacramento stuck. A drafted street plan resulted in a grid of twenty-six lettered and thirty-one numbered streets.

The names of the main rivers in the area—Feather, Yuba, and Sacramento—came from Spanish explorers, except for one: the American. Ironically it was anything but "American" in origin. Spanish-speaking Indians referred to Canadian trappers, most likely those of the Hudson Bay Company, as Americanos. The place where these trappers crossed one stream they called El Paso de los Americanos. Sutter shortened the name to "American." Thus the one river with a truly national designation turns out to have been Spanish in origin, named for Canadians.

River as Depository

In what became standard practice throughout American history, from the first New England towns to those of the advancing frontier, all kinds of waste, including deadly chemicals from riverside paper and woolen mills, and later factories, were routinely dumped into rivers. What happened to the waterway and its inhabitants was of little concern. It was no different with the Sacramento.

The river initially served the very people who would later flush poison-laden residues into it. At first it was the Golden Highway, transporting hordes of gold-seeking "argonauts" (the name given to Jason and his followers searching for the Golden Fleece). In just one month in 1849, more than six hundred vessels carrying would-be miners left San Francisco by boat for the gold fields.

Horse- and cattle-drawn wagons stood ready in Sacramento to carry them east to the foothills or north to the upper valley. Sacramento's population burgeoned from 2,000 in 1849 to 9,000 by 1850. That autumn it became the first incorporated city in the state.

The stampede for gold nearly decimated the Native Americans, who lost first their lands and then their lives. It also was not kind to John Sutter. Tens of thousands of greedy interlopers and squatters trashed Sutter's land and crops, and butchered his animals. Partners cheated him. Creditors hounded him. Workers got gold fever and left. By 1852, New Helvetia was thoroughly wrecked. Bankrupt, Sutter left Sacramento and spent the rest of his life seeking compensation for his losses, to no avail.

In the gold madness, waterways and mountains were devastated. Harnessing the power of water proved most lethal. In 1853, two miners built a wooden contraption held together by iron clamps that could channel water down a slight gradient through a canvas hose. The force kept building until unleashed at a small opening at the end of the hose—literally a blast of water shooting out as if from a cannon. The process was called "hydraulic mining," the delivery mechanism a "monitor." It took a single monitor only a few hours to dislodge far more earth than a team of miners working many weeks with picks and shovels.

This technique kept becoming more powerful. Through the use of increasingly narrow pipes, the water soon was being blasted out at a staggering 130 feet per second, equal to five thousand pounds of force. Landforms that developed over millions of years were changed in days to muddy debris, most of which wound up in the nearest river or stream. With gravity providing free energy, monitors ran around the clock. Reservoirs were created to store huge quantities of water carried by a vast network of flumes constructed on canyon ridges and hillsides. Untold timbers were used for fuel, flumes, mine supports, and structures in the numerous mining towns springing up across the foothills. Entire mountainsides of old-growth trees were denuded, causing them to erode under heavy rains and send even more debris into canyons and waterways.

The runoff carried tons of rocky substrate and mud laced with mercury, arsenic, and other poisonous minerals—"slickens"—through the canyons like massive volcanic lava flows. It filled and choked waterways, widened and altered channels, buried bushes and trees, and

raised stream- and riverbeds as much as one hundred feet.

The reign of terror was unrelenting. In 1875, late spring and early summer mountain runoff combined with slickens went roaring down the waterways, heading inexorably toward the Sacramento Valley. The towns of Marysville and Yuba City, sitting below the Feather and Yuba rivers, were swamped. Marysville was buried as though in a large coffin. Another flood happened five years later, sending surges of rolling liquid muck and rocky debris downriver, sweeping barns and ranch houses off their foundations, covering fruit and nut trees, and killing horses and cattle. Former hillsides in the Sierra Nevada covered the valley floor.

Farmers cried to the government for help, to no avail. California's government was in its infancy; mining still reigned supreme. The primary beneficiaries of this destruction were the owners of mining companies, water companies, real-estate moguls, and even wealthy investors in Britain. The rich were getting richer; everything else be damned. And there were no laws to stop it.

The influx of slickens devastated the Sacramento River. Water loaded with mercury and arsenic poisoned the water, its creatures, and its plants. Tons of sediment buried the river's natural substrate, wiping out fish spawning beds and delicate plant life. It filled in channels, bays, sloughs, vernal pools, and wetlands all the way to San Francisco Bay. Shipping ground to a halt.

It turned out that hydraulic mining produced far less profit than warranted. Mountains were being pulverized for skimpy flakes of gold. Close to seventy thousand gallons of water were being used to recover only a dollar's worth of low-grade gold deposits. To deliver this water, approximately 5,300 miles of flumes, canals, and ditches were built, the length of a coast-to-

Double stacker gold dredger used in rivers to uncover gold. From the Special Collection of the Sacramento Public Library.

coast road and halfway back again. No longer could such costs be dismissed as necessary, albeit regrettable, consequences of huge economic benefits. But what tipped the balance was what was happening to farming communities.

In August of 1878, angry farmers formed the Anti-Debris Association to take on powerful mining interests. They organized a seventy-man militia to protect the valley. For their part, mining companies argued they were there before farmers and possessed legal rights, including that of "dumpage" into waterways.

In September 1882, an owner of farmland in Marysville, Edwards Woodruff, filed an anti-debris lawsuit against one of the titans of the mining industry. The case, *Edwards Woodruff*

v. North Bloomfield Gravel Mining Company, was heard in U.S. District Court in 1884 before Judge Lorenzo Sawyer. In 1863, Sawyer had been elected to the California Supreme Court, serving until 1869, when President Ulysses S. Grant named him to the Ninth Circuit Court, the first federal judge from the Pacific Coast.

In a verdict that changed the course of American law, Sawyer ruled in favor of Woodruff, finding that hydraulic mining represented "a public and private nuisance." He further ruled that the industry's discharges adversely impacted navigable streams and rivers. The judgment reverberated across the Sacramento Valley, prompting celebratory fireworks, marching bands, and bonfires.

The Founding of Redding

T HE DISCOVERY of gold in Coloma by Sutter employee John Marshall prompted another of Sutter's employees, Major Pierson Reading, to order Indian workers on his ranch along the Sacramento River in the northern valley to start panning for gold on nearby Clear Creek. Reading had previously ventured north at Sutter's behest in 1845 and established an outpost—Rancho Buena Ventura—on lands he acquired from the Mexican governor.

Pierson B. Reading.
Gold seeker and developer.
Shasta Historical Society.

Reading proceeded to run steamboats up the river to a place called Latona, near the mouth of Clear Creek. There he planned to build a town that he intended to call Reading. This was the farthest reach of shipping on the river, but his attempt was short-lived as there were too many obstacles in the waterway above Red Bluff for large boats to navigate, despite Reading's numerous and expensive efforts to make the channel more hospitable.

The discovery of gold on Clear Creek and other nearby tributaries to the Sacramento River, as well as on the Trinity River, changed everything. Hundreds of would-be miners swarmed to the region, establishing settlements throughout the area. The largest was a town that surprisingly came to be called Redding.

Although it was Pierson Reading who triggered initial growth in the region and became known as the "Father of Shasta County," it was Benjamin B. Redding for whom the town was named. In 1872, Redding, a former California secretary of state, sent a survey crew to the region to lay out a town site north of Red Bluff for the California & Oregon Railroad. When the town was laid out, instead of being named Reading as intended, the foreman of the survey crew named it Redding after his boss.

Benjamin B. Redding.
Politician, railroad agent,
and conservationist.
Shasta Historical Society.

Major Reading's friends objected and in 1873 had the legislature restore the name to Reading. But in order to please the railroad, a petition came before the legislature to repeal the act of 1873 and change the name back to Redding, which was done.

Besides his work for the railroad, B.B. Redding was a staunch conservationist who initiated the State Board of Fish Commissioners, forerunner of the Fish and Game Commission. Thus, it is the town's rich fishery legacy, rather than its destructive gold-mining past, that is highlighted by its final namesake.

The Sawyer Decision, the first major environmental decision in the United States, upheld a doctrine traceable all the way back to the Roman Empire—the "Public Trust Doctrine." It holds that certain common properties, such as rivers, oceans, and air, are held by the government in trusteeship for the free and unimpeded use of the general public. Private interests may not damage or threaten such common properties. Sawyer's landmark decision laid the groundwork for future decisions involving threats to the common properties of humankind.

But by this time, mountains and waterways had been thoroughly damaged, much of it irreversibly. Hydraulic mining had blasted some twelve billion tons of earth out of the mountains, eight times what was dug to construct the Panama Canal. Much of this was dumped into the Sacramento River.

Harnessing the River

Those who came to the Sacramento Valley to settle rather than temporarily mine for gold apparently ignored the dangers of living in a floodplain. Yet the Sacramento River flooded repeatedly, as it had for eons.

The Indians knew of the river's infrequent but predictable flooding and accepted it. In locating villages close to the river, they chose elevated spots when they could. And their dwellings were not made to last, unlike those of the settlers who constructed one- and two-story buildings right on the river's shores. Yet signs of past flooding were everywhere: high-water marks and dried mud high in trees; eroded hillsides; driftwood scattered far inland and in the crotches of trees; tales of men sailing over what was now the city.

When surging river water engulfed the city of Sacramento in early 1850, it should not have come as a surprise. But the flood caught residents totally unprepared. The major surge of water arrived late at night. The swelling American and Sacramento rivers rose at the rate of six inches an hour and created a huge sea. By morning, hundreds of residents were perched on housetops in dire need of help. The streets remained flooded for a week; people could get about only by boat. Sacramento's one hospital was underwater, and many residents died.

The city eventually dried out, but more water was in store. March brought unseasonably warm weather, which caused mountain snowmelt to thunder down tributaries and into the Sacramento River, once again inundating the city.

Two major floods only months apart convinced Sacramento's residents flooding was not just a freak event and that some kind of levee system was desperately needed. The first levees were three feet high and extended from Sutter's New Helvetia to the American-Sacramento junction. Initially they kept storm waters at bay. But in 1852, another monster storm overwhelmed the levee system and left Sacramento resembling Venice. In the mountain canyons the torrents swept away flumes, tools, buildings, water wheels, and everything that was not securely fastened. Much of this eventually got swept into the Pacific Ocean, where passing ships saw the flotsam for weeks.

The 1852 flood dramatically exposed the levee system's inadequacies and the ongoing risk of flooding. Nonetheless, Sacramento was made the state capital in 1854.

A decade passed without floods. Then in the winter of 1861–62, two torrential storms slammed the valley, and raging waters again breached the levees. The first storm, in early December, set the first recorded high-water mark. After a brief respite, the heavens unloaded deluges that went on for a month, setting a new record. Once more a vast inland sea was

Flooded Sacramento streets, 1861-1862. From the Special Collection of the Sacramento Public Library.

Brick walls used to raise streets in Sacramento in the mid 1800s are still visible in Old Town, Sacramento. Bob Madgic.

created throughout the Central Valley, this time extending as far as Southern California. Only the tops of the Sutter Buttes showed above the water.

It was now clear the city needed more than just levees to protect it. In an audacious scheme, business and civic leaders decided to raise the foundation of the entire city. In 1864, workers began building brick walls up to fourteen feet high on both sides of every street. Wagons hauled in thousands of cubic yards of earth to fill in between the walls. New sidewalks covered the gaps between the raised streets and adjacent buildings. Wealthy owners jacked up their buildings so first floors would be at the new street level; other owners kept their first floors as basements, still vulnerable to high water. When the next big flood came in 1867, the strategy worked: the streets stayed above water. But the full containment of flooding remained an elusive goal, as later events would show.

Sacramento became known as an indomitable city. This reputation was formalized when civic leaders placed the Latin inscription *urbs indomita* on Sacramento's city seal.

River as Provider

In the midst of the gold frenzy, some turned to an enterprise with more lasting potential— agriculture. The earliest endeavors featured sheep and cattle ranching; the shortage of workers and irrigation systems precluded little else.

At first, the Sacramento Valley discouraged farming. Beyond the riparian forests and wetlands were plains of hard dirt where only stunted alkali grasses sprouted each spring. This was good for livestock but little more. "Cattle barons" ruled. Slowly, fields of wheat and other grains that required little or no irrigation took root. By the second half of the nineteenth century, wheat fields carpeted the valley, creating a waving sea of grain. California soon led the

nation in wheat production, shipping it as far away as England, Mexico, China, and Chile.

By the late 1800s, fewer than one hundred men—the "Kings of Wheat"—owned 1.6 million acres in the valley. Most lived elsewhere and cared little about the soil's long-term fertility. Without fertilization, soil nutrients were used up until only unsightly stubble remained. A prolonged drought and crash in wheat prices caused the large grain ranches to dry up and later be subdivided into smaller parcels.

At the same time, budding agrarians began planting fruit and nut trees and crops. They set their orchards and fields close to the river and drew water from it. They improved irrigation systems and employed steam-powered farm machinery. To expand the amount of arable land, settlers leveled tens of thousands of acres of riparian forests and savannah. Lumber mills began to prosper. More levees were built to protect farmlands. In due time, orchards and crop fields dotted the valley.

This growing agrarian economy attracted more and more people, including Easterners. Fed by the Sacramento's water, the region sprouted into the nation's so-called "fruit and nut basket." Towns like Chico became noted for almond and walnut orchards, and Corning—the Olive City—for its olive orchards.

Most astonishing was the explosion of rice farms. The initial impetus came from thousands of rice-consuming Chinese immigrants who came to California during the gold rush. Farmers started growing rice for this market. After this group was banished by the 1882 Chinese Exclusion Act, immigrant Japanese farmers and investors drove the fledgling industry. These "rice barons" knew the hard alkaline soil and moderate climate optimized the growing of rice. They diverted thousands of acre-feet of water from the Sacramento River to their clay

A bird's eye view of the Sutter Buttes. Bruce King.

"Snow specks." Several species of geese continue to feed on crops. Bruce King.

Farmlands provide habitat for waterfowl today. Mike Peters.

fields, converting them to rice paddies. By 1915, 720,000 sacks of rice were being produced, valued at $1.5 million. A year later the total had jumped to 2.5 million sacks, valued at $5 million. Although the Oriental Exclusion Act of 1924 halted Japanese immigration, the crop was there to stay.

Today the California rice industry produces over two million tons of rice annually, second only to Arkansas in this country. Rice contributes in excess of $1.3 billion to the state's economy, more than ninety-five percent of it from the Sacramento Valley. Rice farmers have long burned residue rice stalks. By law this air-polluting practice is being incrementally reduced until all burning ends. They now keep fields flooded for as long as eight months at a time. These surrogate wetlands have almost quadrupled the bird habitat formerly in place. This has helped duck populations to increase,

delighting hunters who pay to hunt on the rice fields, and rice farmers who have found a new source of income.

River as Highway

Early on, the Sacramento River carried logs to sawmills that sprang up during the lumber boom of the gold rush. Oxen, which were plentiful in the region from having pulled covered wagons west, were used first to haul timbers out of forests. Being slow, they were replaced by horses and mules. Later, steam traction engines were used to pull "big wheels," sometimes eight feet in diameter and connected by an axle where logs were strung. (These giant machines left ruts in bedrock where they traveled, some still visible today.) Flumes, many as long as forty miles, were built to carry rough-cut lumber from mountain sawmills to the valley floor.

Steam ship and passengers in the heyday of steamboats on the river. Courtesy of Rio Vista Museum.

Awaiting the logs were river riders and huge rafts made of large timbers bolted together. Often as many as twenty rafts were joined, held together by wooden pegs tamped into deep auger holes cut into the planks. The riders—"river rats"—navigated them downriver through swift currents and rapids. The cargo and rafts were sold in Marysville, Sacramento, and other destinations. After unloading the timber, the raftsmen took stagecoaches back to prepare for another river journey.

The timber-rafting era was a brief one, as rafts were soon supplanted by the railroad and other means of transport. Meanwhile, the river was becoming a major artery for boats and ships. As it did for logging, gold spurred shipping and related industries like fish packing. At first the few boats plying the waters were slow schooners powered by small motors and sails. The first steam-powered boat on the Sacramento River was the *Sitka*, a tiny thirty-seven-foot

boat built in Sitka, Alaska. It was disassembled there and reassembled in San Francisco. In the winter of 1847 it left for Sacramento, a trip that took almost seven days. Although the *Sitka* sank the very next year, it introduced a new way to power ships.

The first passenger steamboat on the Sacramento was the *George Washington*, which began regular service in August 1849. It was followed by the more powerful *New World*, which made the trip from San Francisco to Sacramento in six hours, ushering in the "age of steam." Soon river boats became "floating palaces" with plush interiors, sumptuous food, and calliopes.

Some ships not only steamed to Sacramento, but kept going upriver to Red Bluff, the farthest destination for large boats. From there, pack trains and stagecoaches transported passengers, particularly miners, northward. By 1854, nineteen steamships were docking in Red Bluff, causing businesses there to sprout and grow.

Paddleboat at dock in Red Bluff, the farthest destination for large boats. Courtesy of Tehama County Genea-logic and Historical Society.

Newly built homes reflected the Victorian architecture popular in San Francisco. Despite times of low water and high costs to keep the river navigable, Red Bluff continued to thrive as a shipping destination up to the time the Sacramento River ceased being the valley's major transportation artery.

One of the most famous early river steamers was the *Antelope*. Five hundred and fifty feet long, it carried up to three hundred passengers. By the early 1850s it was the fastest and most reliable steamboat on the Sacramento River. The *Antelope* left San Francisco precisely at 4 P.M. and departed Sacramento at 2 P.M. the next day, completing each leg in exactly eight hours. Because of the *Antelope*'s regularity and reliability, the Wells Fargo company chose her to carry enormous quantities of gold each week to San Francisco.

The *Antelope* also carried the first Pony Express mochilla (Mexican saddlebags) from Sacramento to San Francisco. Inaugurated on April 3, 1860, the Pony Express's first delivery was from St. Joseph, Missouri—the western end of rail and telegraph—to Sacramento. It took ten days with sixty-mile riding stints for each horseman. From Sacramento, the *Antelope* carried the mail to San Francisco, arriving near midnight to large crowds and a spontaneous parade. The cost of a single letter was five dollars for the eighteen-hundred-mile trip, making the Pony Express a losing venture. The laying of copper wires for telegraph transmission, which reached California in 1862, ended the Pony Express's short life.

The *Antelope*'s notoriety made other ship owners jealous and combative. Captains of bigger paddlewheelers intentionally crashed into her sides. One individual built a steamboat, the *Sacramento*, expressly to challenge the *Antelope* for speed. To keep potentially angry passengers in check during this heated river battle, all passengers were required to turn in their revolvers upon boarding. The episode ended with the *Antelope* ramming the *Sacramento* and pushing her broadside down the river for a short but humiliating distance.

The riverboat *Chrysopolis*, launched in 1860, was a customer favorite. Called the "Slim Princess" due to her sleek design, she set a long-standing record of five hours and nineteen minutes between Sacramento and San Francisco. Her schedule was so punctual that people along the way reportedly set watches by her passage.

Riverboat disasters were common. Faster steamers attracted the most passengers, so captains wanted maximum speed. In narrow, un-

marked channels, boats jockeyed for position, crowding each other and sometimes colliding. Captains zigzagged to prevent other boats from passing. For more speed they used volatile fuels like pitch or oil along with wood in the boilers, which sometimes exploded. One notorious calamity struck the *Washoe* in 1864. On the river below Rio Vista, her boiler blew up, ripping decking into thin kindling and hurling burning wood and shattered iron everywhere. Scalded people leapt into the river. More than half of the two hundred passengers died.

Gold mining initially spurred boat traffic, then stifled it by smothering the river with sediment. In places it raised the riverbed twenty feet, causing boats to hit bottom. More levees were built to raise the water level. Up to this

The steamer Valletta *passing the Colusa bridge, May 1908. The multi-span bridge, which was replaced in 1980, had a hand-operated two-span swing unit with a Pratt truss. The opening mechanism is now on display at nearby Colusa Levee State Park.*

The Delta King *sits today at Old Town Sacramento where it serves as a hotel and restaurant. Bob Madgic.*

point they were often built only on the developed side and spaced far from the river, which allowed it to fan out and meander. The new levees were built closer to the river and on both sides, squeezing the channel tighter and raising its level, thus providing clearance for ships.

In 1869, Sacramento became the western terminus of the transcontinental railroad, which further boosted shipping. Luxurious steamers awaited train passengers. Joining the steamers were stern-wheelers—flat-bottomed boats that could go in shallower waters. These small carriers made frequent stops along the river, dropping off passengers and merchandise from San Francisco. On return trips they picked up fruit, vegetables, hay, and other farm products for merchants in the city.

Another vessel was the "store ship." These so-called "floating variety stores" carried items to small and remote communities, blasting a distinctive whistle to announce their arrival.

Residents would often barter for goods, offering fruit, dairy products, potatoes, and sometimes even a pig, calf, or crate of live chickens in return for manufactured items.

River navigation slowed during drought years and when too much mining debris from spring floods clogged the river. During a string of low water years and heavy irrigation withdrawals in the 1920s, the Sacramento had almost no outflow at its mouth. A cut was made at Horseshoe Bend at the entrance to the Delta to flush out mining debris and sediment and substantially improve navigability.

As farm production increased, more boats were needed to carry the increased tonnage. Commercial boating reached its peak in 1925, when close to a million and a half tons were moved. Once railroads began to dominate both cargo and passenger transportation, the glory days of boating on the Sacramento ended. As more of a romantic link to the past, boats like

The Sacramento Deep Water Ship Channel was built in 1963 to accommodate ships to the Port of Sacramento, shown here. Bob Madgic.

the *Delta King* and the *Delta Queen*—the largest and fastest stern-wheelers ever to ply the Sacramento—provided luxurious overnight passenger service between Sacramento and San Francisco into the 1940s. The *Delta King* was then bought and sold several times; parties fought over its ownership in court; twice it sank and had to be rehabilitated; and it was located variously in Richmond, Stockton, and as far away as Seattle. In 1986, it was brought to the dock in Old Town Sacramento, where it still serves as a restaurant, hotel, and tourist attraction.

In addition to historic boat traffic, the Sacramento was also home to another vintage form of river travel—ferries. A myriad of scows and barges—each with its own power source— hauled livestock, loaded wagons, and humans across the river.

In 1963, to accommodate large boats going to and from Sacramento, the U.S. Army Corps of Engineers completed the "Sacramento Deep Water Ship Channel," a separate canal-like channel about thirty feet deep, two hundred feet wide, and forty-three miles long. The Port of Sacramento remains an important shipping nexus, primarily for agricultural products like rice and other bulk goods.

The River and the Arts
The Sacramento River's distinctive images and places have long inspired artists, writers, film producers, actors, and hucksters.

In the latter half of the nineteenth century,

stern-wheelers were sometimes transformed into showboats that stopped at small communities along the river. Theater groups that included actresses Lola Montez and Lotta Crabtree presented shows in community facilities or aboard the ship itself. They were often joined by "medicine shows," in which con artists peddled miracle cures for varied ailments and personal improvement.

Writer Bret Harte based his 1868 book *The Luck of Roaring Camp* on the great Sacramento flood of 1862. It made him the best-selling author of his time. One of Harte's contemporaries was Samuel Clemens, who adopted the name "Mark Twain," a riverman's term for water just safe enough for navigation. Twain wrote travel accounts for the Sacramento *Union* newspaper in 1865, the same year his short story, "The Celebrated Jumping Frog of Calaveras County," was published, launching his career as one of America's most notable authors.

Twain's connection to the Sacramento River persisted after his death in 1910. Early movie versions of two of his most famous books, *The Adventures of Tom Sawyer* and *Adventures of Huckleberry Finn,* were filmed along the Sacramento, which was used to represent the Mississippi River. Author Julian Dana notes that the Sacramento doubled for many rivers in early film scenes: yellow pirates battling over red decks on the Yangtze; a horse and rider daring death in an Ohio floodtide; red men in canoes hunting scalps along Virginia's James; spike-booted hemen tossing logs and villains about on the Columbia. The film *The Good Earth* was also set on the Sacramento, with scores of Chinese farmers serving as actors in this story about China.

Before 1935, at least forty-five feature-length movies were filmed in the Sacramento area, more than half of them using Delta waterways to depict the Mississippi River. Transforming a Sacramento steamer into a Mississippi steamer only took a bit of plywood and an extra smokestack. This was the case in a 1959 version of *Adventures of Huckleberry Finn,* with a cast that included Tony Randall, Judy Canova, Andy Devine, Buster Keaton, Archie Moore (as Jim), and Eddie Hodges (as Huck).

~

The resolve of the Spanish and Euro-Americans who first came to the Sacramento River was tested in untold ways. Native Americans fought to defend the land; river navigation proved daunting; and flooding occurred far more often and with far greater consequences than the first settlers foresaw. But these newcomers and those who followed worked to overcome each obstacle and fully utilize the river's resources. They settled the Sacramento Valley and built towns and cities—including one that became the state capital. An agricultural mecca sprouted in place of wetlands, riparian forests, and hardpan plains.

Even as the river provided vital nourishment, its very essence was transformed, primarily by the building of ever-larger levees. Deplorably, the "taming" of the Sacramento River was also accompanied by poisonous gold-mining materials being discharged into its waters. But the transcendent Sacramento River would eventually heal and continue to provide sustenance, its waters and wildlife deemed more precious with each succeeding year.

Mossbrae Fall on the Upper Sacramento River above Dunsmuir. A foot trail to it is being built. Bob Madgic.

CHAPTER FOUR
The Upper River

*"Springs of medicinal waters, the blend of minerals stored
away in the volcanic age of Shasta, issue from the cliff on the
left bank, and other springs burst out in torrents many rods
in width that leap to join the river over walls of columnar
basalt or large faces of malachite and azurite."*

—*John Powell Irish, 1888*

THE ESSENCE OF THE UPPER SACRAMENTO River watershed is an abundance of pure, cold water, like that found in few other places on earth. It gushes out of the ground and from moss- and fern-covered hillsides; it runs and ripples in the clearest of streams; it plunges and cascades over rock walls; it spurts from surface cavities; it bubbles up laden with minerals; it tumbles and gurgles over stones and logs; it splashes crystal baubles and sprays gossamer mist; it roars down the canyon, crashing and swirling over and around rock gardens; it gathers in the greenest of pools, before surging forth once more.

The native peoples knew the value of water. The Wintu Winnemem—the middle river people—considered water their birthplace. Their lifestyles and culture, like those of other Indian tribes in the region, centered on the river flowing near their villages and on the creatures these rivers supported. Water was sacred.

It took the white person much longer to reach this conclusion. For a long time, little thought or effort was given to conserving water

and using it prudently. Eventually that would change, for as an (anonymous) individual has stated, *all the water there will be, is.*

Siskiyou Trail

Before the white man came to the region, native peoples used a trail that followed the canyon river. The Wintu, who called the river *nom-te-mem,* or "river over the hill," occupied its lower stretches. To the north lived the Okwanuchu, members of the Shasta Indians. Being mainly nomadic, the Wintu and Okwanuchu used the canyon trail when hunting or fishing, and for visiting other villages.

In the 1830s, fur traders and their horses enlarged the pathway. In 1834, an ambitious cattleman from Oregon named Ewing Young—a member of the new Willamette Cattle Company—secured (likely stole) some 150 horses and mules from Mexican ranchos and California missions and began the six-hundred-mile return journey. For three months, the Oregonians drove the animals up the canyon, trampling vegetation and widening the trail.

Sheer rock walls that alternated sides forced numerous river crossings. Once Young reached Oregon, authorities wouldn't let him sell possibly contraband livestock. Nonetheless, he had shown that such a venture was possible.

Three years later, Young returned to California by boat and with cash. He purchased 729 cattle in San Francisco at three dollars per head and 40 horses at twelve dollars each. He and his workers then launched another drive back to Oregon. In the Sacramento Valley they endured drought, sweltering heat, and dwindling food. By the time they reached the river canyon, both man and beast were suffering.

In what has been called the great cattle drive from California to Oregon in 1837, the group made it to the Willamette Valley in five months. They lost 100 cattle and 25 horses. The men ate one cow, and Indians killed a few; the others either died or disappeared. The investors sold the cattle for $8.50 per head. The cattle drivers were paid $1 per day, payable in cattle. Expenses for the trip totaled $42.75.

The rugged pathway—named the Siskiyou Trail—soon became the major route between California and Oregon. It exploded in usage with the discovery of gold north of Mt. Shasta in 1851. A mule driver named Abraham Thompson noticed a gold glint in a tuft of grass dislodged by one of his animals. When word got out, some two thousand prospectors traveled the trail to get there. A settlement known as Thompson's Dry Diggings (later named Yreka) sprang up. Soon it was bustling with saloons, dance halls, banks, and hotels, and what one writer called "a mixed and motley crowd—a restless, roving, rummaging, ragged multitude." Miners ultimately took an estimated $60 million worth of gold from the grounds, making it by some accounts the richest square mile in the world.

Prospectors also found gold in waterways throughout the region, including the main stem of the Sacramento and its tributaries. Mining settlements multiplied, the first being Shenanigan's Gulch, better known as Portuguese Flat (located near today's Pollard Flat on the Upper Sacramento River). One of the wildest mining camps in California, it mixed gold, whiskey, and Indian women.

In the mid-1850s, an enterprising explorer named Ross McCloud transformed the Siskiyou Trail to a wagon and stagecoach road linking the gold-mining towns of Shasta City (today's Old Shasta) and Yreka, seventy-five miles to the north. The road sometimes stayed alongside the river; other times it was cut out of the steep forested hillside. The workers built seventeen bridges in forty-three miles, with the road crisscrossing the river canyon.

As gold fever raged, the region's natural beauty also captured attention. One spectacle difficult to ignore was Mt. Shasta. Poet and traveler Joaquin Miller called it the Monarch of Mountains and wrote, "As lone as God, and white as a winter moon, Mount Shasta starts up sudden and solitary from the heart of the great black forests of Northern California.... I implore you go prepared to see and comprehend, so far as possible, the indescribable calm of this colossal Shasta world. The soul grows there."

Miller's words resonated. The glorious mountain attracted the adventuresome, sightseers, and some of America's foremost artists, including Albert Bierstadt, Thomas Hill, and William Keith. By the close of the nineteenth century, Mt. Shasta had become the second most popular subject in California behind Yosemite for artistic renderings.

Among the notables drawn to Mt. Shasta was John Muir, who was interested in studying its glacial formations. In multiple visits, he climbed to its summit three times. This remarkable man walked up the river canyon from

Redding to Mt. Shasta (after first arriving in California, he walked from San Francisco to the Sierra Nevada). When he initially spotted Mt. Shasta in 1874, he related, "When I first caught sight of it over the braided folds of the Sacramento Valley, I was fifty miles away and afoot, alone and weary. Yet, all my blood turned to wine, and I have not been weary since."

Most of those who traveled the river corridor did so by stagecoach. By 1859, a weekly stagecoach service, carrying passengers and mail, ran between Sacramento and Portland, Oregon. By 1872, there was daily service between the fledgling towns of Redding and Roseburg, Oregon.

A stagecoach ride on the windy, bumpy road, with numerous river crossings and unpredictable weather, was often a harrowing experience. The "mud wagons" often flipped. Passengers sometimes fired their pistols at bears, mountain lions, and other wild creatures. Marauding Indians and outlaws posed constant danger. The infamous Black Bart—Charles E. Boles— allegedly robbed stages between Yreka and Sacramento in the 1870s and early 1880s. (He was finally captured in San Francisco in 1883.)

The fifty-mile trip between Redding and the small town of Sisson at the base of Mt. Shasta was a twenty-four-hour ordeal. Passengers often arrived exhausted, filthy, and sick to their stomachs.

Arrival of the Railroad

The coming of the iron horse ended the twenty-five-year stagecoach era. The California and Oregon Railroad first laid tracks from Sacramento to Redding in 1872. This spurred Redding's growth, but lack of funds stymied railroad expansion northward. By 1885, rail construction had restarted, with the Southern Pacific Railroad Company taking over the lease. Work began on a rail line up the river canyon, largely following the Siskiyou Trail.

More than 7,000 men—including 5,000 Chinese immigrants—bludgeoned the canyon with machinery and dynamite. The line crossed the river eighteen times, with thirteen tunnels blasted through the hillsides. Explosives and huge steam shovels gouged out tons of dirt and rock that clogged the river. For food or just for sport, workers threw sticks of dynamite in the river to kill fish. Although all rivers have a remarkable ability to heal, the Upper Sacramento River—the "Upper Sac"—and its corridor were forever changed.

After more than forty miles of carving up the canyon and laying track, the workers reached a flat area, followed by a steep incline. A single engine towing cars could not climb the grade there. "Pusher" engines were needed, prompting the start of a small railroad center that built and serviced the engines. Before long it grew into a small town named Pusher or Poverty Flat. Its name was later changed to Dunsmuir, after a coal baron from British Columbia named Alexander Dunsmuir who donated a fountain to the town.

The most rugged section, just before Box Canyon, still lay ahead. In the narrow confines, the river made a wide, sweeping loop, stumping the surveyors on where or how to place the rail line. Whether fact or fiction, the solution presumably came from a sheepherder, who wandered by to bum tobacco from the workers. Pondering the puzzle, he told officials they needed to make a big turn across the river and go up the other side. This became the infamous Cantara Loop crossing—a fourteen-degree loop at the eighteenth and final crossing of the river.

To complete the move, a train coming up the river's western side had to make a sweeping hairpin turn over a trestle bridge, then backtrack and gradually work its way eastward. Another hairpin curve at the top of the canyon

The river canyon is still the railroad route for trains heading north or south. Bob Madgic.

got the train going northward again. Train engineers were tested: too much speed entering the Cantara Loop could cause derailment and a plunge into the river; too little speed and the train could not climb the grade. Trains heading south went only two to three miles per hour on the steep downward grade. Passengers often disembarked, walked down a trail, and reboarded the train farther down the track.

Above Box Canyon, the canyon gave way to a valley flanked by Mt. Shasta and Mt. Eddy. From there the railroad track pushed northward to Portland.

The completed rail line represented a remarkable engineering achievement. A visitor from England described a train trip up the canyon: "Following the canyon of the Sacramento river from the south, the way of the train is 'the way of a serpent on a rock.' Slowly gliding against the heavy grade, winding in and out the interminable curves, diving into innumerable

tunnels, crossing and recrossing nearly twenty bridges, in only rather more than as many miles, now with the music of the rushing river at one window, now at the other, and always the towering spires of the pines bristling against the near skyline above, the journey in itself through this rugged part of the country is well worth the doing, well worth the increase of fare, which here amounts to some six cents a mile."

The railroad dramatically impacted the region. In 1892, a lumber mill was built near the Cantara Loop, necessitating a cable tram to retrieve timber from the steep hillsides. In the nearby town of McCloud, the new Valley Railroad Company—forerunner to the McCloud Lumber Company—constructed a rail line deep into a nearby forest. Flat rail cars hauled timber back to sawmills in McCloud. Milled wood was sent by rail to a box factory in Sisson, a burgeoning lumber-based boomtown. By the early 1900s, the McCloud Company owned ten engines and three hundred cars and had constructed seventy miles of railroad. Farther to the north, a man named Abner Weed purchased 280 acres and constructed a mill in 1897. He also founded a town and named it after himself.

At that time, fifty-two sawmills operated between Dunsmuir and Weed. Some of the finest stands of old-growth sugar and ponderosa pine trees in California were cut in the region, including far up the slopes of Mt. Shasta. Log skidders, steam tractors, and teams of oxen, horses, and mules removed the logs. Monoculture tree "plantations" filled in the now-denuded ancient forests.

People would learn in time that trees and forests were as finite as gold and other minerals. The only enduring constant in the region was water.

Discovering the Power of Water

Facilities for travelers lined the Siskiyou Trail well before the railroad arrived. Small hotels, inns, saloons, stores, and even farmhouses provided services for those making the journey. One farmhouse was Fry's, located at Soda Springs, fourteen hours by stage from Redding. It was billed as "a clean, comfortable little mountain inn, where you could get good and well-cooked food and a comfortable bath," all especially welcomed by weary stagecoach travelers.

When one guest asked whether there was still gold in the area, Mr. Fry reportedly went to his garden and uncovered a few specks of gold by scraping in the dirt. He said that when he planted his apple trees, he found quite a bit of gold. But the old miner opined that "a good apple orchard is more profitable, in the long run, than a poor gold mine." Left unsaid was that an orchard needs water, an understandable omission given Fry's proximity to the river.

The railroad revved up passenger traffic. Whereas a stagecoach could carry a handful of people, the railroad could transport hundreds. Southern Pacific Railroad advertised aggressively. It billed the line as the "Road of a Thousand Wonders," promoting majestic Mt. Shasta, the cool river canyon, and its striking surroundings—including Castle Crags, a formation whose massive splintered granite spires framed the river like a "crumbling medieval castle."

It wasn't long before the region's abundant, pure, cold spring water—and its profuse "mineral" and "sparkling" water—also became major draws.

Although all water contains minerals, the water in the Upper Sac had unique volcanic origins. When hot magma erupted from Mt. Shasta eons ago, massive streams of lava flowed down mountainsides and into the Sacramento River canyon. Incinerating everything in its path, it filled the canyon and buried the river for more than forty miles to depths of seventy-five feet. Once the lava solidified, resurgent water flowed over its surface. Over time, a revived river carved a new canyon. Underground water, quite probably the old river, seeped through the lava and burst forth as springs and waterfalls. As the water surfaced, it possessed a wide array of minerals that rendered it distinctly supra rich.

This water paradise boasted varied strata and flows, with elements and taste differing from source to source.

At the outset, tourist places were built near springs. In the 1850s, a resort named Bailey's—later renamed Lower Soda Springs Resort—featured "soda" or "seltzer" water. Joaquin Miller recommended that travelers to Mt. Shasta should "make your first, if not your final, stopping place at Lower Soda Springs. This spring is of itself, to say nothing of its fabulously invigorating waters, a curious study. Besides that, it is the first spot ever occupied by the white man in all its region."

The Southern Pacific Railroad Company put out posters like this one to attract customers. Provided by College of the Siskiyous.

Shasta Springs Resort was one of many early resorts that accommodated tourists who wished to "take the water." Provided by College of the Siskiyous.

Upper Soda Springs Resort followed. Located near the last northbound crossing of the Sacramento River, Wintu called the site *Memokis-takki*, meaning "strong water place." Two brothers built a cabin and stables there to host travelers. It later became a more substantial inn, with a covered springhouse for the public to enjoy the "soda water."

Within a decade of the first train chugging up the canyon, at least fifteen other water-related resorts dotted the Upper Sac. These included Sisson's, Shasta Springs, Shasta Retreat, Castle Crags Tavern, Castle Rock Springs Hotel, Ney Springs, and Cave Junction. The railroad delivered thousands of travelers to these places, many to escape the stifling heat of the Central Valley. Others came cross-country—and some from as far away as Europe.

Guests came to stay a week, a month, even all summer. Many of the well-to-do in this Victorian Era, particularly the elite of San Francisco, considered these inns and lodges their retreats. Wealthy Californians like the Stanford, Crocker, and Hearst families built vacation houses in the region. Celebrities—including Mae West, Jimmy Dorsey, Lena Horn, and Cary Grant—visited frequently. One popular gathering spot was a Castella resort and bar.

The most famous resort was Shasta Springs Resort, just north of Dunsmuir. Railroad workers first built a drinking fountain there to capture the naturally carbonated spring water that gushed out at twenty gallons a minute. After the railroad arrived, Southern Pacific constructed a station, fashioned a gazebo over the springs, and built a large platform so passengers could mill about, drink the water, and visit the gift shop. Promotional literature claimed that

Postcard showing visitors enjoying the "healing water" at Shasta Springs. Provided by College of the Siskiyous.

"these springs…are certain to take their place with the very best drinking water in the country.…"

Soon every passenger train was stopping at the resort. Although a drink of the fabled water was gratis, money was squeezed from tourists by charging for an "aluminum, collapsible, sanitary, souvenir drinkin' cup."

To accommodate overnight guests, Southern Pacific built a large hotel and cottages on the bluff overlooking the river. A cable tram carried a dozen guests and tourists at a time up the steep hillside. Non-hotel guests paid five cents for the thrilling roundtrip ride, reportedly called "one of the best five-cent rides of its time."

In 1889, a company calling itself the Mt. Shasta Mineral Springs Company built a bottling plant on the resort's premises. Soon it was shipping the famed "Shasta Water" from Portland to Los Angeles. Demand for the bottled water soon outstripped supply. Water was then shipped in railroad cars to the San Francisco Bay Area, where it was re-carbonated and bottled. The company—which changed its name to the Shasta Water Company—then began filtering tap water and calling it "Shasta Water." Except for the name, this was the company's last tie to Shasta Springs.

Tucked among Shasta Springs Resort facilities were signs reading, "Shasta Water for Health." As it turns out, this was not a novel idea. From the beginning, each resort favorably situated sought to capitalize on the therapeutic benefits of "taking the water."

Water as Healer

People had long believed in the restorative power of water. The founder of Bailey's (Lower Soda Springs Resort), for instance, had been an invalid for four years prior to his arrival in the area. Physicians couldn't cure his ailments, but by drinking the sparkling water at the springs, he claimed to have "regained his wonted health." The Bailey family went on to promote their resort as having "the finest mineral waters in the State, if not in the United States. In twenty-two years there has not been a single case of malaria, unless it was contracted elsewhere and brought to the place in the system."

In another case, a Mr. Steward was ailing and on the verge of death. Native Americans brought him to mineral waters a few miles north of Mt. Shasta. After he soaked several times, his health returned. He established a rustic resort at the springs—Stewards Mineral Springs Resort—featuring "healing waters."

Lured by the health benefits, tourists came to drink the water, soak in it, and enjoy the region's clean air, forests, and river sounds, therapeutic in their own right. Many believed the water cured a range of ailments, from emphysema to rheumatism, and that it helped with kidney functioning, digestion, heat reduction, and intestinal and bowel activity.

Indicative of prevailing views, a local newspaperman wrote: "…it [water from Mossbrae Falls] is most effective if one or two glasses be taken in the morning from twenty minutes to one-half hour before breakfast; the same before lunch and dinner and likewise before retiring for the night."

Some of the mineral water was delightfully flavored; some of it smelled and tasted bad. One writer noted that "…in every sip, one is conscious of the chlorides and iodine, the carbonates and bi-carbonates which are at its base. Having once tasted, one is not so eager to join the throng the next time he passes this way."

The region's aqueous offerings also included sparkling carbonated water. Such natural "soda water" results from carbon dioxide gas (CO_2), a common feature in subterranean rocks in lava regions. One traveler noted how these springs differed. Soda was so extensive in one, she reported, that its water could be used instead of yeast or baking powder to make bread. "Flour mixed with it rises quickly and nicely," she observed.

Resort owners put their own spin on their water. One promoted its sparkling water as "aiding the flow of saliva, and allaying gastric irritation." Another claimed that its waters "are highly recommended for their medicinal properties." Others just touted the "Famous Water," or "the purest of ice water."

Some resorts began adding artificial flavor to their soda water. The *Dunsmuir News,* for instance, reported in 1891 that a certain resort "will manufacture a first-class article of lemon-flavored drink from the soda water and sell it to train passengers at five cents a glass."

Perhaps the most enterprising resort was Ney Springs Resort. While hunting, John Ney and a companion had stumbled upon mineral springs, from which flowed Stink Creek. After buying property there, they shrewdly changed the name to New Springs and launched Ney Springs Hotel. Two miles from a railroad stop, it featured a spectacular eighty-foot waterfall named Fairy Falls and a bathhouse for soaking in the mineral water. Resort literature said it contained "carbonate of magnesium, bicarbonate of sodium, and carbonate of calcium. It also contains lithium, iron and arsenic in perceptible amounts; in all 19 ingredients, of which all but three are mentioned as traces. It may be drank freely at all times with beneficial results."

Ney bottled the water and sold it for medicinal and beauty applications. The label for its "Aqua de Ney" read in part: "This water has been experimented with, used and applied for the cure of stomach and blood diseases for more than twelve years…. *Aqua de Ney* has an odor peculiar unto itself, and it must be confessed this odor is not as agreeable to the olfactory as

lavender; but it disappears in a few minutes."

For its "Beauty of Water," the label read in part: "'*Beauty of Water*' has been used and applied for about four or more years as a shampoo, face-wash and lotion. It has also been used for the cure of cutaneous diseases."

It was clear that the rich supplies of water in the Upper Sacramento River watershed could be exploited in many different ways, and that such exploitation was in its infancy.

Attraction of the Rainbow

The region boasted an additional form of wealth besides gold and water. In the tumbling waters of the Upper Sac—and its tributaries, the Mc-Cloud and Pit rivers—lived one of California's most fabled natives: the rainbow trout. A direct descendant of the sea-run rainbow or steelhead and one of America's most beautiful fishes, this rainbow strain has a greenish-yellowish hue, densely black spotted body, and a brilliant scarlet stripe running along its sides.

The rainbows were resident wild trout, meaning they were born and lived in these waters. The self-sustaining population was estimated to be nine thousand fish per mile, as prolific a trout fishery as existed anywhere. With remarkable clarity, the oft-swift-flowing river combined shoots, ripples, and deep pools. It flowed over and around rocks and boulders of all sizes, smoothed from centuries of erosion and polish. As the water tumbled and crashed, it churned in gushes of whitewater. Rainbow trout—*Oncorhyunchus mykiss ssp*, a member of the coldwater salmonid family—evolved and thrived in this cold, highly oxygenated, mineral-rich water.

Rainbow trout possessed far greater value than most people at first realized. For many they were a handy and cheap source of food. An early observer, for instance, noted how some of the streams actually ran under houses. If a busy housewife had neglected to prepare anything for dinner, "all she needed was to open a trap door in the floor, put in a colander with some meal scattered on the surface, and pull up one or two flapping trout ready to clap into the frying pan."

Angling's growing popularity brought new appreciation for the species. When hooked,

cept of a "limit" on how many one could keep was unheard of until the early twentieth century, when a cap of twenty-five was established for a day's fishing—still a generous allotment. Huge numbers of trout were removed from the river, presumably to be consumed.

For others, fishing became more a sport than a food-gathering mission. Methods soon

A Sacramento River rainbow trout. Allan Craig.

the rainbow is a tenacious fighter, leaping high out of the water and then streaking for safety. The thrill of hooking one captivated more and more people, who began coming to the Upper Sac primarily to fish. The railroad and resorts soon touted the outstanding fishing in addition to spring water. A highly dubious story even spread that a train passenger could stick a fishing rod outside the window on a stop near the river and hook a trout. To promote this rumor, the Southern Pacific Company in fact may have placed trout in the most convenient pool for this very reason.

In this era, fish populations were generally seen as limitless. Anglers measured success by the number of fish on their stringers. The con-

reflected this emerging outlook, in particular those of fly fishing—the use of artificial "flies" that mimic bugs that trout eat. By seeking to imitate insects and their behavior, the fly fisher seeks to be part of the trout's world. Plus, hooking a fish with a fly usually occurs in or around the fish's mouth instead of in its belly, like with bait. The fish is less likely to die and can be returned to the water. The purist fishes strictly for the joy of the hook-up and releases all fish that he or she catches.

An early renowned fly fisherman on the Upper Sac in the early 1900s was a Wintu man named Ted Towendolly. A later disciple was Ted Fay, who perfected his own method for hooking rainbows. He tied heavily weighted flies

Etching of Thomas Hill's painting of anglers on the Upper Sac. Provided by College of the Siskiyous.

that resembled organisms being swept down the river: black and brown flies, caddis larvae, caterpillars, and yellow jackets, among others. He used two flies at once, placed about twelve inches apart. Then, using a staff, he waded aggressively out in the river to where rainbows mainly held: in gushing water just upstream or below rocks where water tumbled and swirled—"pocket water." With a short line, he sunk his two weighted flies deep down in the churning water, hopefully right where a trout held waiting for food. Reportedly, Fay once caught seventy-six fish in two hours, and also remarkably hooked two fish simultaneously on each of five casts, for a total of ten fish.

Ted Fay recognized that the population of rainbows in his river was finite and that the vast numbers of fish being caught and killed every year had to take a toll on the fishery. An early advocate of conservation, he began practicing "catch and release," while urging fellow anglers to "limit your kill, don't kill your limit."

The nearby McCloud River was also renowned for its native rainbows. It was the only river in California where native bull trout—also called dolly varden—existed. (The species is now extinct in the McCloud and state). Unlike the Upper Sac, no public resorts were built alongside the river. But many wealthy individuals and private groups, mainly from San Francisco, purchased riverfront property. The newspaper baron and builder of castles and mansions, William Randolph Hearst, acquired over sixty thousand acres along the McCloud, for example. He built an extensive retreat resembling a Bavarian village that he called "Wyntoon" after the Wintu Indians. In the lower section of the river, two private fishing clubs purchased wide expanses of riverfront land: the McCloud River Club and the San Francisco-based Bollibokka Club.

With the rich fishery in these waters, interest developed in propagating fish for distribution elsewhere. In 1872, Livingston Stone built the Baird Hatchery on the lower McCloud to raise salmon, primarily to send eggs to the East Coast (see the next chapter for more on this). It was growing rainbow trout that really took off, however. In the 1880s, a federal hatchery on the McCloud started breeding them, shipping the eggs throughout the world. The Sisson Hatchery, built in 1888, also began by raising salmon. By the early 1900s, it, too, was rearing rainbow trout—the "Shasta rainbow." The progeny of these rainbows soon spread to waters across the country, such as in eastern and Rocky Mountain states, and in faraway New Zealand, Chile, and Argentina.

While the love affair between anglers and the Upper Sac watershed grew, the advent of auto travel changed other facets of the region. The popularity of staying at a resort and "taking the water" dissipated with multiple driving vacation options available. As decades passed, fewer visitors came, and resorts started closing. Businesses related to fishing became the lifeblood of local economies. Among tourists and adventurers, interest in Mt. Shasta would only grow.

Although currents were shifting, the flowing water remained constant. Gathering from its many sources, it pushed toward its destination. Once there, transformed from its long journey, the water would be returned to Mt. Shasta and Mt. Eddy, there to refurbish the many springs and rivulets that once more would collect and surge down the river canyon.

All the water there will be, is.

Presidents and the Upper Sacramento

THE BEAUTY and natural richness of the Upper Sacramento River region got the attention of the nation's leaders. In the 1880s, President Rutherford B. Hayes took a stagecoach to Sisson, stayed in the Mount Shasta Hotel, and marveled at the beauty of Mt. Shasta and other sights.

President William Howard Taft, an avid fly fisherman, visited in the early 1900s. He stayed in the Eagle Inn in Castella and fished the river.

In May 1903, President Theodore Roosevelt traveled by train up the Sacramento canyon, stopping first in Dunsmuir. Here a large crowd gathered to greet "Teddy." The train also stopped at Sisson, where Roosevelt gave a short speech. He later wrote that the evening twilight on Mt. Shasta was "one of the grandest sights I have ever witnessed." Two years later, Roosevelt established the Shasta National Forest.

In October 1919, President Woodrow Wilson rode the "President's Special" down the canyon. It stopped at Shasta Springs, where he drank from the springs and visited nearby Mossbrae Falls. The train made another stop in Dunsmuir, where the president was presented with one hundred choice rainbow trout caught in the Sacramento River that morning. (It's not clear what he did with the trout.)

A long-standing rumor, verified by locals, is that President John F. Kennedy came to the region for a tryst with Marilyn Monroe, presumably staying in a cabin in Castella. Monroe reportedly signed her name in lipstick at a bar that has since disappeared.

In 2004, George H.W. Bush—with a party that included his wife, two grandchildren, and former British Prime Minister John Major—traveled up the Sacramento canyon in a special train dubbed No. 41, in honor of the forty-first president. Vince Cloward of the River Exchange served as his guide. The train made a special stop at Mossbrae Falls. The president, an angler, wondered about the fishing in the river. To entice him to come back and try it out, Cloward presented him with a collection of Ted Fay flies. (Bush did not return.)

President Theodore Roosevelt addressing a crowd in Dunsmuir in 1903. Provided by College of the Siskiyous.

Shasta Dam and the vast lake it created. Department of Water Resources.

CHAPTER FIVE

River Transformed

"Aridity, and aridity alone, makes the various Wests one… And what do you do about aridity if you are a nation accustomed to plenty and impatient of restrictions and led westward by pillars of fire and cloud? You may deny it for a while. Then you must either try to engineer it out of existence or adapt to it."

—*Wallace Stegner*

WALLACE STEGNER, EMINENT WRITER on the West, noted that the only exception to the region's aridity, apart from moisture-laden mountains, is in the very northwestern areas. Even California is largely a semi-desert. And when the heavy rains do come, primarily from San Francisco northward, they fall in the winter, not in the growing season.

What Stegner didn't address was what happened to precipitation after it fell. Before human alterations, Sacramento Valley rainfall was often augmented every winter and spring by torrents of water from the upper watershed and melting snow gushing down the river's tributaries, regularly flooding the valley and sometimes creating a gigantic inland sea. Extending one hundred miles from the Sutter Buttes to the Delta, and from the Sirrra foothills to the coastal ranges, this was one of America's largest freshwater wetlands. It took months for the water to drain into the San Francisco Bay.

In the vast Los Angeles Basin, meanwhile, average annual rainfall totaled only fifteen inches, with few other sources of water available. Inland sat the San Joaquin Valley, historically a stark, desiccated landscape of dry grasses and cracked earth. Stegner's prognosis applied: both regions were destined for a parched future unless humans engineered aridity out of existence. The remedies for both regions lay in water from the north.

The stage was set for the Sacramento River to be transformed. First its unrelenting and overpowering force had to be tamed and contained so humans could safely and productively live and farm in the Sacramento Valley. And secondly, if the Central Valley and Southern California were to bloom into gardens and metropolises, its water had to be taken.

Battling the Inland Sea

The first levees built in the mid-1800s protected the Sacramento Valley most of the time. But severe flooding still happened. One posited remedy was building even larger levees. Another was to have excess waters bypass the main channel.

Although the Great Inland Sea is now history, the Sacramento Valley still experiences widespread flooding. Chadd Santerre.

The Sutter Bypass was once a natural channel that received flood waters from the Sacramento River. It does so again today. Bob Madgic.

Year after year the matter went unresolved, and episodic flooding continued to ravage valley dwellers. Some communities and farmers fortified their lands with makeshift levees—little more than mounds of dirt—and pushed the floodwaters over to the other side. Those on the newly flooded side then reciprocated

major bypasses—the Sutter Bypass and the Yolo Bypass—among many other contrivances.

In the Sutter Basin a natural flood channel once existed, but levees prevented historic inflows from entering it. Two new weirs first contained the waters and then released it into this broad channel—the Sutter Bypass—as nature

The Yolo Bypass and weirs shown here were constructed to prevent flooding of the city of Sacramento. Walt Simmons.

in "guerrilla warfare," pitting neighbor against neighbor. As author Robert Kelley reported in *Battling the Inland Sea*, such internecine conflict went on for decades. A masked party once rowed across the river, overpowered guards, and cut open a disputed embankment, allowing the river to flow through its normal overflow channel. Those protected by the embankment rebuilt it, only to have its enemies mount another naval assault.

Such anarchy couldn't continue if the entire valley was to be safe from flooding. Massive floods in 1907 and 1909 overwhelmed the levees yet again, finally prompting the Sacramento River Flood Control Project. It featured the construction of more levees, weirs, and two

intended. The excess water flows down the channel and re-enters the river near the confluence of the Feather and Sacramento rivers, home to a major portion of the Sutter National Wildlife Refuge.

The Yolo Bypass addressed the sweeping section of the river below the city of Woodland above the city of Sacramento—that included a vast tidal marsh known as the Yolo Basin. (The name Yolo is derived from the Native American name Yo-loy, meaning "a place abounding in rushes.") In winter it was a shallow, tule-filled swamp, an oasis for many species of birds and animals but inhospitable for humans. It also impeded land travel between San Francisco and Sacramento. Newly built weirs rerouted excess

Levees along Sacramento River in 1950. From the Special Collection of the Sacramento Public Library.

floodwater via the bypass around Sacramento and returned it back to the river above the city of Rio Vista. When inundated, the area is nearly a third the size of San Francisco and San Pablo bays with a water depth of roughly ten feet.

As reported by Kelley, the Sacramento River Flood Control Project included 980 miles of levees; 7 weirs or control structures; 3 drainage pumping plants; 438 miles of channels and canals; 7 bypasses, 95 miles in length, encompassing 101,000 acres; 5 low-water-check dams; 31 bridges; 50 miles of collecting canals and seepage ditches; 91 gauging stations; and 8 automatic shortwave-radio water-stage transmitters.

Such reconfigurations radically transformed the river. The torrents that created the inland sea were now thoroughly checkmated, the half-

million acres of swamplands "reclaimed," the ecology of the Sacramento Valley forever altered. As Kelley writes: "The Sacramento and its tributaries are [now] hidden behind a thousand miles of high levees, massive in their bulk, which have made a Holland of the Sacramento Valley."

Sending Water South

While the inland sea was being conquered, the middle and southern parts of the state struggled with water scarcity.

The parched San Joaquin Valley rested in the center of the Golden State. By the early 1900s, some wealthy farmers and irrigation districts had cultivated only a few parts of the valley. What radically changed the region were cheap oil, electricity, and the motorized centrifugal pump, all of which made pumping water from the ground both feasible and cost-effective. And, according to water scholar Marc Reisner, "…finally freed from all constraints but nature's, the farmers began pumping in the finest California tradition—which is to say, as if tomorrow would never come."

By 1930, groundwater was irrigating a million-and-a-half acres, supporting fruits, dairy products, cattle ranches, and crops, including two of the thirstiest—cotton and alfalfa. Not surprisingly, as farmers pumped more groundwater, the water table dropped, in some places by nearly three hundred feet. As the water table sank, so did the land, a process called "subsidence." Subsidence in excess of one foot and up to twenty-eight feet had affected more than 5,200 square miles of irrigable land—one-half the entire San Joaquin Valley. To offset these deficiencies, farmers demanded water be brought to them.

To the southeast sat the Los Angeles Basin. The main surface water there was the Los Angeles River, a largely seasonal, meager waterway. Any substantial water existed underground. As described by Reisner: "Everyone was living off tens of thousands of years of accumulated groundwater, like a spendthrift heir squandering his wealth. No one knew how much groundwater lay beneath the basin or how long it could be expected to last, but it would be insane to build the region's future on it."

So two of California's regions sat poised for growth, one in agriculture, the other in people. Relying on groundwater in both places meant future bust. All eyes turned to the watersheds of the northern half of the state.

Central Valley Project
The unequal geographical distribution of California rainfall did not go unnoticed. Early studies plotted north-to-south water transfers, but they led nowhere. In the 1920s, however, the "California Central Valley Project" was designed and approved, mainly at the behest of politically powerful San Joaquin Valley farmers. The project would capture water from the Sacramento and San Joaquin rivers and transport it southward through thousands of miles of canals, making it the biggest water project in history. All it required was money.

The stock market crash of 1929 wiped out any hope of state financing. It fell to newly elected President Franklin Delano Roosevelt (FDR) to rescue the project. After first visiting Shasta County in 1932 to promote his New Deal, three years later he ordered the Bureau of Reclamation to take over the Central Valley Project, which would include a massive dam in Shasta County.

County officials wanted a dam on the Sacramento to control flooding and irrigate orchards. Ranchers and fruit growers blocked a proposed dam in the Iron Canyon area of Tehama County. Influential stalwarts like Judge Francis P. Carr, Roscue Anderson, and dairyman John McColl pushed for a large dam where the Sacramento, McCloud, and Pit rivers joined in the deep canyon above Redding. They successfully lobbied FDR to have the federal government build such a dam.

The 1930s materialized into the glory days of dams. Boulder Dam, later renamed Hoover Dam, was the first of the colossuses. Completed in 1935, the primary beneficiaries of the diverted Colorado River water via the Colorado Aqueduct were California's Imperial Valley and the Greater Los Angeles area.

Up north, no sooner had FDR approved the Central Valley Project than he approved the Grand Coulee Dam on the Columbia, where construction of the Bonneville Dam was already underway. So, by the end of the 1930s, each of the country's four largest dams—Hoover, Bonneville, Grand Coulee, Shasta—was either built or about to be.

The logic behind dam building at the time was compelling. Not only had the nation's financial markets collapsed, but irresponsible farming practices in the Southwest and a prolonged drought created yet another national calamity—the Dust Bowl. FDR sought to create jobs through public works programs, and few rival the building of dams for mega expenditures. (This so inspired legislators that hundreds of dams were constructed in the 1950s and 1960s—the "age of dams"—as politicians stampeded to bring federal dam projects—"pork"—back to their districts.)

Many at the time saw dams as actually advancing conservation—John Muir, among others, would have vehemently disagreed—since what better way to conserve water than to store it? By "saving" water that otherwise would be "wasted" if it flowed directly to the sea, it could not only irrigate distant farms but also *when* they needed it most. Dams created hydroelectric power, so much so that the kilowatts generated by the Grand Coulee Dam alone almost gave America sufficient energy to defeat the Nazi war machine. And dams controlled flooding, at least some of the time.

Shasta Dam

All of this logic applied to the dam that would forever alter the Sacramento River—Shasta Dam. And despite what its first proponents stated, the overriding reason for it was clear, as put forth by regional scholar Dr. Al M. Rocca: "The main purpose in its construction lay in the attempt to solve California's historic water problems. Shasta Dam and the resultant Shasta Lake would become the 'keystone' of the Central Valley Project." Another part of the project would be Friant Dam and the resulting

Millerton Reservoir, to be built on the San Joaquin River. Both Shasta and Millerton would store water to deliver to California's thriving agribusinesses, many of which were eventually dominated by big corporations like Chevron, Tejon Ranch (one of the great land empires of California), Getty Oil, Shell Oil, and Tenneco.

Left out of the decisions on dams were Native Americans, particularly the Winnemem Wintu whose villages and sacred sites would be lost to the massive Shasta Lake. (Some compensation was given to Wintu landowners.) Little thought was given to the loss of salmon and other migratory fish in the Sacramento and San Joaquin rivers, or to the degradation of the rivers themselves. No value was given to sections of free-flowing rivers and wild canyons that would be gone forever. The forces behind dam building faced little opposition—environmental groups were basically non-existent at the time—so all of these countervailing factors were conveniently ignored.

Given the southern transfer of Northern California water, it's a wonder Shasta County officials wanted a dam so badly. The answer was simple: economic opportunity. Like the rest of the country, Shasta County was in the throes of an economic bust. Gold mining was nearly exhausted, and a major copper-mining boom basically ended with World War I. As it turned out, this mining boom primarily made absentee investors wealthy, while leaving in its wake scores of unemployed residents, crumbling towns, poisonous residues, and an earth stripped of life.

With the onset and then unrelenting grip of the Great Depression, all parts of the country were desperate for economic revival. The construction of a massive dam held great promise for Shasta County's economy. As preparations got underway in 1937, hordes of workers arrived

The Ravages of Copper Mining

WHEN OPERATIONAL, smelters from Shasta County's copper mines—two of the biggest were Keswick near Iron Mountain and Kennett in the Sacramento River canyon thirty miles above Redding—filled the air with toxic sulfide smoke that devastated vegetation for miles around, including orchards twenty miles away. In his book, *Murder of a Landscape,* Khaled J. Bloom states that twenty years of airborne poisons followed by twenty years of fire and rain had completely devastated more than two hundred square miles—forty times the territory seared by the Hiroshima A-bomb.

The damages to human health, largely undocumented, were also horrific. And once-clear mountain streams like Spring Creek became "viscid pools of ugly yellow and gray slime" that oozed down gullies and into the Sacramento River. Despite heroic efforts to contain runoff, seepage of the "most acidic water found on earth" continued to enter the river, killing trout and salmon for decades.

Tailings such as these from Iron Mountain contain toxic elements that used to enter the Sacramento River before being contained. Bureau of Reclamation.

Beyond the acidic water, poisonous tailings from the mines have been a devastating residual problem for the region, where they are leached from the open wounds of the hills and carried down waterways. In 2010 alone, the Environmental Protection Agency dredged and removed 175,000 tons of mining tailings from the Spring Creek arm of Keswick Reservoir. Such tailings historically have been pumped back to a disposal pit behind Spring Creek Dam, which was built to keep the metals from entering the Sacramento River.

Today Iron Mountain remains one of the most toxic Superfund cleanup sites in the country.

Mining seepage like this flowed into the Sacramento River. Bureau of Reclamation.

A decommissioned railroad tunnel served as the river channel while the dam was being built. Bureau of Reclamation.

The Sacramento River canyon was thoroughly made over to provide for construction of Shasta Dam. Bureau of Reclamation.

by rail, rundown vehicles, and on foot; they slept in trailers, tents, flimsy lean-tos, and autos. More than a quarter were from Dust Bowl states. Soon "Arkies" and "Okies" were treading about Redding, to the dismay of locals. Camps and towns like Toyon, Shasta Dam Village, Project City, Summit City, and Central Valley, along with dormitories, mess halls, makeshift

canyon walls of impenetrable vegetation, then jack-hammering and dynamiting bedrock to create a huge depression. In some areas, Native American and other gravesites were dug up and their remains moved to new graveyards.

To allow for dam construction, more than thirty miles of railroad track had to be moved. This required the building of many bridges,

What remains of the town of Kennett, shown here, now sits at the bottom of Shasta Lake. Bureau of Reclamation.

hospitals, and schools, quickly grew to accommodate a wide array of personnel and, in some cases, their families.

The superintendent of construction was master dam builder Frank Crowe. He had just finished his crowning achievement—Hoover Dam. Affectionately known as "Hurry up Crowe" and "The Old Man," Crowe made Shasta Dam his finale.

Initially the dam was going to be called Kennett Dam after the once-thriving town soon to be inundated by the new lake. The name was later changed to Shasta Dam to honor the majestic mountain visible in the distance. At 602 feet tall, it would be among the largest dams in the world. The work entailed first clearing

trestles, and tunnels, including one through the hillside to detour the train temporarily around the dam site. The permanent solution lay in constructing a bridge over the Pit River high enough to be above the new reservoir. Completed in 1942, it was the highest railroad bridge ever built in the country.

The Sacramento River then had to be diverted away from the work site. It was shunted into the decommissioned railroad tunnel, while a concrete abutment kept the river contained in its new straitjacket. Now the dam could be built where the river once flowed.

The work required enormous quantities of cement, gravel, and sand. Cement was trucked from the Kaiser Permanente Plant in the San

At Turtle Bay, gravel was gouged out of the river and sent nine miles via conveyor belt to the dam site.
Bureau of Reclamation.

Francisco Bay Area, 250 miles away. The best gravel was 10 miles away in the Sacramento River (where today's Redding Convention Center and Turtle Bay Exploration Park are located). It was excavated from deep in the river's bed. A giant "grizzly and jaw crusher" mashed the gravel, and the world's longest conveyor belt—9.6 miles—carried it up to the dam site, taking one hour and forty minutes. In four years of operation, the belt carried more than 12.2 million tons of sand and gravel, enough to fill 244,000 railroad cars in a train 2,080 miles long, the distance from San Francisco to Chicago.

The dam's construction design consisted of 16,900 massive concrete blocks, fifty-by-fifty feet each, and five feet deep. The amount of concrete eventually used to build the dam was enough to build a sidewalk around the earth's circumference.

Workers earned on average ninety cents an hour—the norm elsewhere in the country was twenty-five cents an hour—for the highly dangerous work, particularly the "highscalers," who, anchored by ropes, hung and clung like spiders to the steep canyon walls, or later, the smooth sides of the growing concrete monolith. There were no nets to catch someone who fell. (Fourteen workers lost their lives during construction.) Work proceeded seven days a week, twenty-four hours a day, with lights illuminating the site "like a gigantic circus," as one observer noted.

The Sacramento River's final flows before being blocked by Shasta Dam. Bureau of Reclamation.

In 1940, massive rains and flooding halted the work. February saw torrential deluges, six inches in just four hours. The river roared down the canyon, thundering at 185,000 cubic feet per second (cfs) past the dam site. (Normally 50,000 to 100,000 cfs is considered flood stage.) The raging water overwhelmed the diversion channel. On March 29 it rained another 9.2 inches, the highest amount ever recorded there in a twenty-four-hour period. When the river finally receded, deep mud covered everything. The gravel site in Redding was a lake. Parts of the conveyor belt and its bridges were ripped apart. Cleanup and repair lasted until July. All told, it rained 108 inches that year, almost double the normal amount.

If construction and weather challenges weren't enough, World War II exploded. Since the dam would produce hydroelectric power, it was considered a war project, exempting workers from military service and rendering them "veterans." Nonetheless, many left to join the armed forces, replaced in part by women and older teens. Some feared sabotage by Japanese-Americans or an out-and-out attack on the dam by enemy planes. Soldiers guarded the site;

other security personnel patrolled around the clock. (With the benefit of historical perspective, the dam never really was at risk from these elements. This kind of national hysteria led to America's most deplorable violation of civil rights: the internment of Japanese-Americans in relocation camps.)

Efforts intensified to finish the dam. The last bucket of concrete was poured on December 22, 1944. Before Shasta Lake was filled, timber and other remnants were salvaged from the town of Kennett. Bulldozers or fires demolished what remained. As rising water eclipsed any remaining vestiges, one stubborn resident, Lawrence Bannon, refused to accept the loss of his home and community. He lived on a houseboat where the town used to be and commuted to work by motorboat. (It is not known how long he did so.)

Frank Crowe retired after Shasta Dam was completed, intending to live as a rancher in Shasta County. Two years later, he died of a

heart attack. A simple gravestone in a Redding cemetery marks the burial site of this man who greatly influenced the region. It reads: "Frank T. Crowe—Builder."

The smaller Keswick Dam was built nine miles down from Shasta Dam, as an afterbay impoundment that further controls water releases and generates power. Completed in 1950, it created Keswick Reservoir, which sits at the foot of the toxic Iron Mountain.

Shasta Dam spurred the growth of Shasta County and especially Redding. After World War II broke out, its turbines produced 625,000 kilowatts that powered ship-building plants and aircraft installations. Beyond hydroelectricity, the dam's other benefits include flood control, water storage, improved river navigation, regulation of salinity levels, and new recreational opportunities.

One dubious benefit attributed to the dam was that it "promoted fish conservation." Given that it blocked salmon and steelhead runs

Houseboating is highly popular on Shasta Lake. John Gantner.

Another widespread activity on Shasta Lake is water skiing. Bob Madgic.

from their historical waters, thus threatening them with extinction, Shasta Dam was hardly a stroke for fish conservation. (It did create a spectacular tailwater fishery of wild rainbow trout, but that's a story for another chapter.)

With the dam in place, the Bureau of Reclamation controls all releases and flows in the Sacramento River. The dam captures high water runoff during the wet winter months, stores it, and then releases it during the agricultural growing season—late spring through early fall—opposite the natural regimen of the river that historically saw high winter flows and low summer flows. It's a matter of computer and human calculations: if too much water is released without compensatory refilling, Shasta Lake recedes; too little water released accompanied by unexpected massive inflows from heavy rains risks downriver flooding. The maximum release from the dam is 79,000 cfs. Any amount over that means the water is going over the dam—something the Bureau wants to avoid at all costs.

To some, Shasta Dam is tantamount to a living goddess. One Bureau of Reclamation officer wrote: "[Shasta Dam] represents more than a monolith of strength, indeed more than a wonderment of science. At times it is as if She whispers a marvelous and wondrous story. In the silence of late afternoon, She tells Her story as the evening shadows dance across Her face, brings to life what the casual observer might mistake as lifeless concrete.... She tells of the unleashed fury of nature that for centuries unrelentingly scoured Her canyon walls with ravaging floodwaters, sent thundering into the valley below to baptize all within its bounds, and then, as if to tantalize, would withhold the life-giving stream when needed most to quench the scorching thirst of the valley...."

There were less fanciful depictions. When the dam was completed, superintendent Frank Crowe was quoted in *Time* magazine as saying, "That meant we had the river licked, pinned down, shoulders right on the mat. Hell, that's what we came up here for."

With the Sacramento "pinned down," it would never again be a true and complete natural river. The primary beneficiaries of this artificial makeover were agribusinesses in the San Joaquin Valley, as intended. Yet, even Shasta Lake and the new Millerton Reservoir on the San Joaquin—completed in 1942—did not provide enough water to satisfy those down south.

Seizing Trinity River Water

Although the Trinity River flows on the other side of mountains from the Sacramento, in a convoluted way it became one of its tributaries, or a facsimile of one, and another major piece in the Central Valley Project.

Headwaters of the Trinity River originate deep within the rugged Trinity Alps Wilderness, roughly 500,000 acres of jagged peaks, deep-cut valleys, and forested landscapes. Scattered deep among the 6,000- to 9,000-foot peaks are more than fifty-three alpine lakes and countless bountiful springs. This vast watershed at one time delivered its full bounty to the Trinity Basin and Trinity River, which flowed uninterruptedly before joining the Klamath River 130 miles downriver. Like the Klamath, it was a prime waterway for migrating salmon and steelhead. Native American tribes such as the Hoopa Valley and Yurok depended upon these fish, which also provided anglers with spectacular recreation.

Far to the south in western Fresno and Kings counties sits Westlands Water District, encompassing more than one thousand square miles.

The Trinity River at one time was a pristine river replete with wild salmon and steelhead. Ken DeCamp.

Penstocks carrying Trinity River water over the mountains for deposit in Whiskeytown Lake. Bob Madgic.

About fifteen miles wide, it stretches seventy miles from Mendota on the north to Kettleman City on the south. Average annual rainfall is seven inches, and as California historian Kevin Starr writes, "the soil was baked by the sun to such hardness that it frequently has to be broken with dynamite." Impermeable clay lies beneath this upper crust. Until the 1960s, Westlands was largely a desert wasteland, sprinkled with a few arid ranchlands and struggling farms drawing on groundwater. Then, quite amazingly, the fates of Westlands and Trinity River conjoined.

As agribusinesses and politicians sought more southern water and hydroelectric energy for the Central Valley Project, valley representatives lobbied for the creation of a Westlands Irrigation District, arguing it would create six thousand "family farms" that would help feed California and the nation. They set their sights on the bounteous water of the Trinity River. Several big Westlands landowners and political contributors swayed ambitious Red Bluff

The Trinity River's water is used to irrigate Central Valley farmlands. Courtesy of Sustainable Living Cotton Project.

congressman Clair Engle to introduce a bill in the U.S. House of Representatives that would divert six hundred thousand acre-feet from the Trinity River and send it to the San Joaquin Valley.

In December 1955, the U.S. Congress authorized the "Trinity River Division of the Bureau of Reclamation's Central Valley Project." It provided for construction of two dams on the Trinity to store water, miles of tunnels and turbines to get it through and over the mountains and into the Sacramento, and hydroelectric plants to generate power. A Bureau of Reclamation official stated under oath to the Congressional committee that "no more than 56 percent of the Trinity's water would be diverted." To mitigate for the loss of salmon and steelhead spawning habitat blocked by the dams, approximately 109 miles of waterways in all, a hatchery would be constructed below the dams. A Bureau official made the standard claim that it "would make the fishery even better than it was."

Upon completion in 1963, the Clair Engle Dam created a huge reservoir called Clair Engle Lake. The smaller Lewiston Dam directly below it created an afterbay impoundment called Lewiston Lake. And then, astonishingly, *ninety percent* of the water from the Trinity watershed was diverted. (This continued for the next nineteen years.) The water is sent via the eleven-mile Clear Creek Tunnel to the Carr Powerhouse at Whiskeytown Lake, another reservoir just west of Redding. Some water is also taken over a mountain by turbines and penstocks and deposited at the powerhouse. From Whiskeytown it is sent via the Spring Creek Tunnel into Keswick Reservoir and the Sacramento River. An equivalent amount of Trinity water is later pumped out of the Delta and diverted to the San Luis Reservoir west of Los Banos. From there it is sent principally to the Westlands Water District.

In losing most of its water, the Trinity River could no longer flood, carve out new channels, scour vegetation, and transport gravel. Its simplified channel grew more silted and restricted by vegetation. The water temperatures increased. The Trinity's natural salmon and steelhead fishery crashed. Nowadays hatchery stock makes up almost ninety percent of the fishery.

In 1984, the U.S. Interior Secretary initiated a study to determine the effect of various water flows on the Trinity's fish and wildlife. He also ordered a reduction in diversions to seventy-three percent while the study was being completed, which amazingly took fifteen years.

In December of 2000, President Clinton's Interior Secretary, Bruce Babbitt, issued a decision that returned about forty-seven percent of total watershed runoff to the Trinity River.

While authorities desperately tried to repair the Trinity, including bulldozing the channel to create more sinuosity, the Westlands Water District was using its water to transform a desert into a garden. The district's main crop was cotton, which provided Westlands with multiple government subsidies—crops, water, and electricity to pump the water. And rather than consisting of "small family farms," many Westlands' owners morphed into corporations or became part of large conglomerate farms.

By the beginning of the twenty-first century, cotton still was the primary crop, but Westlands also became a major producer of tomatoes, lettuce, almonds, citrus, watermelons, pomegranates, alfalfa, and many other nuts and vegetables, all generating a billion dollars annually.

The picture in Westlands is anything but rosy, however. The impervious clay layer underlying the soil prevents irrigation water from draining. The water buildup contains salt, selenium, boron, and residues from pesticides,

Whiskeytown Lake is popular with swimmers, boaters, anglers, and picnickers. Sailing regattas like this one are regular events. Bob Madgic.

herbicides, and fertilizers. In 1981, ranchers discovered deformities and deaths in their livestock, surely attributable to this poisoned water. To solve this problem, the Bureau of Reclamation sent the excess drainage water to Kesterson Reservoir in the valley west of Merced and designated it the Kesterson National Wildlife Refuge. In 1983, U.S. Fish and Wildlife Service officials found that selenium had gotten into the food chain there and was killing algae, plants, insects, fish, and migratory waterfowl. Kesterson was literally a death trap for birds on the Pacific Flyway. In 1987, the site was declared a toxic waste dump and shut down.

When water deliveries to Kesterson stopped, Westlands sued. The district demanded that the government build an extension to an existing canal—San Luis Drain—so that excess irrigation water from their fields could be filtered to the Delta and eventually the San Francisco Bay. In the words of Marc Reisner: "As far as Northern Californians are concerned, the farmers stole all this water from them; now they want to ship it back full of crud."

The matter still has not been settled.

Ominously to some, in 2007, Westlands, already the biggest user of Northern California water, purchased a private fishing club with three thousand acres of land on the McCloud River. Its purposes remain undisclosed, but it's presumed this will facilitate the raising of Shasta Dam—a proposal under consideration—and make still more water available to Westlands.

In response to persistent strong animosity from Trinity County residents toward Clair Engle, Senator Barbara Boxer successfully sponsored a bill in 1997 to have the name of the lake changed to Trinity Lake. Meanwhile, the very hard and expensive work of restoring the Trinity River from its mangled past continues.

California Transformed

Shasta Dam, Trinity Dam, and Friant Dam are only part of a complex maze of reservoirs, canals, aqueducts, pumps, tunnels, and power plants that comprise the Central Valley Project, which starts at Shasta Lake and ends four hundred miles south at Bakersfield. Another major piece is Folsom Dam on the American River, completed in 1955. This impoundment captures the copious waters from the north, middle, and south forks of the American River System and sends it down the Sacramento River, much of it ending up in the Central Valley.

By the time it was finished, the Central Valley Project included twenty dams and reservoirs, eleven power plants, and five hundred miles of major canals, as well as innumerable conduits, tunnels, and related facilities. Ninety percent of this federally controlled water has historically gone to agriculture, helping to create what has been called the "nation's breadbasket"—the richest farm-producing area in the world. If ranked with states for agricultural production, the Central Valley would be fourth, behind Iowa, Illinois, and Texas.

While Northern California water was greening the Central Valley, it was also cultivating brown field workers. From the 1940s into the '60s, an average of one hundred thousand Mexican citizens came to the U.S. each year and provided indispensable seasonal labor. They worked long hours—bending, stooping, reaching, usually under a scorching sun. Earnings were based on quantities gathered or picked, which depended on skill and speed. Many migrant workers stayed in the U.S., including "illegal immigrants," who provided work few others have the stamina and skills to do.

The irrigation of the Central Valley thus helped create the browning of its human landscape. Non-white Californians are now in the majority, with those of Mexican and Hispanic heritage approaching forty percent. Author Richard Rodriquez says, "There is a common society called 'California,' a diverse but emergently ecumenical. The bloodline is incredibly mixed, and we are all Californians. We are becoming more like each other."

In addition to the transformation of the Golden State, the Central Valley Project forever changed the natural characters of many North-

ern California rivers: the Sacramento, American, Trinity, McCloud, and other smaller ones. The next target was the Feather River.

California Water Project

Even before the Central Valley Project was completed, another water project every bit as ambitious and costly was launched in the 1960s. Again the instigators were the agricultural lobby, which requested an inventory of untapped water sources. Not surprisingly, the study expanded to include yet more possible water for Southern California. The dynamics were straightforward: the more water an area got, the more it could be developed. More development attracted more people, which increased demands for more water. At this time California's population was surging, creating what was soon being called the "water crisis."

When Edmund G. "Pat" Brown was elected governor in 1959, his proclaimed mission was to deliver water to Southern California, whatever the cost. He launched a massive water project, later stating, "I wanted this to be a monument to me."

The project was initially called the Feather River Project, but soon became the State Water Project. Its linchpin would be a massive, earth-filled dam on the Feather River, another extensive watershed. Of the river's three water-laden forks, Middle Fork is especially spectacular. It runs and cascades and plummets through a 1,000-foot-deep granite canyon for more than thirty-two miles. Leaving the canyon, it is squeezed between narrow granite walls before thundering over a 410-foot drop—Feather Falls—one of California's most marvelous displays of its most precious asset. Brown's grand design was to use the Feather's water to fuel growth down south, if he could get the project approved. San Joaquin's agribusinesses, many of which were oil companies, were big

The Wild & Scenic Middle Fork of the Feather River plummets 410 feet over Feather Falls. Ray Bouknight.

supporters. Their benefits would include more cars and freeways, generating need for more oil.

In 1955, an enormous flood hit the towns of Marsyville and Yuba City like a tsunami. Some 250,000 cfs of torrential water stormed out of Feather River canyon, sending entire houses

Luis Reservoir, an "off-stream" impoundment. From there, periodic allocations are returned to the aqueduct and on down the Central Valley to Bakersfield. Five pumping stations that require huge energy output move the water over the Tehachapi Mountains. The aqueduct ends

Concrete channels like this carry water from northern to southern California in the 444-mile-long California Aqueduct. Bob Madgic.

downstream. The calamity sealed the deal for the State Water Project.

Oroville Dam was completed in 1968. At 770 feet, it is the highest dam in the country. The resultant Lake Oroville is the second largest reservoir in California, behind Shasta. The captured water is sent directly to the Sacramento River and on to the Delta, where it is pumped into the 444-mile-long "Edmund G. Brown California Aqueduct." After seventy-five miles, the water is pumped up to the San

at Lake Perris in Riverside County. Several offshoot canals supply water to the counties of Los Angeles, San Bernardino, San Diego, and other parts of Southern California.

Upon completion, the State Water Project consisted of thirty-two reservoirs and seven hundred miles of canals and pipelines. Facilities span almost the entire state, from Antelope Lake, Frenchman Lake, and Lake Davis in northeastern California to Lake Perris. To get the project passed, Brown needed to give

The State Water Project involves numerous aqueducts to deliver water throughout California. Department of Water Resources.

something to just about everyone. Bay Area counties—from Napa and Solano in the north to San Jose in the south—receive state water, as do Central Coast counties, all the way south to Santa Barbara. The State Water Project serves more than two-thirds of California's population, with seventy percent going to urban uses, and thirty percent diverted to San Joaquin Valley farms.

Pat Brown did indeed achieve a monument to himself.

~

The complexity of the storage and dispersement of water in the Central Valley and State Water projects boggles the mind. By the time both projects were nearly done—they will probably never be completely finished—California housed 1,251 major reservoirs. Not all were federal and state projects, like the infamous O'Shaughnessy Dam in Yosemite Na-

tional Park that created the Hetch Hetchy Reservoir, which supplies water to San Francisco. Every significant river except for the Consumes and Smith has been dammed at least once. The Stanislaus has fourteen dams on its short run from the high Sierra Nevada to the Central Valley. Largely ignored are water losses due to evaporation in reservoirs and aqueducts, and in seepage from open canals, which combined could be as much as twenty to thirty percent.

Rivers and reservoirs satisfy at best only sixty percent of the demand for water in California. The rest comes from underground aquifers, a finite, non-renewable source. With all of the pumping stations, the energy expenditures just to move water in California rival total energy costs in several states.

As it turned out, adaptation to aridity—as Wallace Stegner had earlier proposed—was never really a viable option.

Fish Introductions

The transformation of the Sacramento River wasn't only about the herculean efforts to control and direct its water. It was also about what was happening in the river itself.

The Sacramento River held one of the richest assortments of native fishes in the world. Other than the magnificent white and green

Coast, where they were considered an outstanding food fish, and placed them in the Sacramento River. Part of the herring family and an anadromous species, the shad navigated to the Pacific Ocean and returned each year in increasing numbers to the Sacramento to spawn. Soon shad were being harvested commercially, an astounding 5.7 million pounds in 1917, for

The introduced American shad is a popular game fish. Dave Allred.

sturgeon, these were mainly coldwater species in the salmonid family, with primordial origins in the Pacific Ocean. These all gave rise to exceptional commercial and sport-fishing opportunities. Fishery managers and ichthyologists believed they could increase such opportunities by importing new species—the more kinds the better.

The food value of fish dominated early fish management. A California State Board of Fish Commissioners was launched in 1870 "to establish fish breederies and to purchase and import spawn and ova of valuable fish suitable for foods."

In June 1871, the commissioners imported ten thousand American shad from the East

example. But Californians never developed a taste for this bony fish, and the market faltered. It remained popular as a game fish.

Another Atlantic Ocean import, striped bass, followed in 1879, again as a potential food fish. Initially, about 135 tiny fish were transported by rail to San Francisco Bay, with little hope of success. But the next year a one-pound striped bass was caught in the bay and a second near Monterey. So another 300 were imported. Within a few years, San Francisco markets were selling large numbers of this popular food fish. Before long, the commercial net catch alone was averaging well over a million pounds a year.

Such successes convinced the fish gurus that any promising species could be stocked in any water, a process called "acclimatization." For example, Stanford president and renowned ichthyologist David Starr Jordan wrote: "A leading feature of the work of the Fish Commissioners must be to help the fishes over the barriers, to assist nature in the direction of colonizing streams and lakes with fishes which are good to eat, to the exclusion of the kinds of fishes which man can make no use."

Before the nineteenth century ended, varied entities had introduced eastern brook trout (1871), brown trout (1893), lake trout (1895), and many warmwater fish species, including catfish, bullheads, black bass, smallmouth bass, carp, yellow perch, green sunfish, white and black crappie, and warmouth. Bluegill and pumpkinseed followed. Attempts were even made to bring Atlantic salmon to West Coast waters, which teemed with Pacific salmon. In 1874, the California Fish Commission imported about 300 small Atlantic salmon from the Penopscot River in Maine and planted them in

Livingston Stone, superintendent of the McCloud River salmon and trout breeding station—the Baird Hatchery—the first one in the country. Livingston Stone Collection.

Collecting salmon eggs from McCloud River for propagation at Baird Hatchery. Livingston Stone Collection.

the Sacramento River near Redding, never to be seen again. Then almost 200,000 Atlantic salmon were hatched from imported eggs in 1891 and released into the Trinity River. Again, no returns materialized. Experimental plantings in several Northern California waters continued up to 1929, all without success.

Hatcheries augmented fish introductions.

purpose was to hatch and rear fingerling trout, salmon, and steelhead—all prized game fish.

By the 1930s, some of the exotic fish imports were producing unintended consequences. Bluegill and other sunfish pushed out the native Sacramento perch from many waters, including the Sacramento River. The voracious lake trout helped eliminate Lahontan cutthroat in Lake

A Sacramento perch, the only native sunfish west of the Rocky Mountains. Bob Madgic.

The first one started when Professor Spencer F. Baird, the U.S. Commissioner of Fisheries, commissioned Livingston Stone of Massachusetts to go west and bring back Chinook salmon eggs. These would be spawned and introduced into East Coast waters where Atlantic salmon were in sharp decline. Stone came to the Baird Station on the McCloud River in 1872, collected and fertilized salmon eggs, and shipped them east by rail. Like the transplanted Atlantic salmon, Pacific salmon didn't survive in cross-coastal waters. But the Baird Hatchery, named after the professor, paved the way for other state, federal, and private agencies to start hatcheries throughout California. Their main

Tahoe by consuming the young cutthroat fish. For a couple of decades acclimatization efforts were halted. But with dams creating ever-new water impoundments, the practice revved up again mid-century. By the 1980s, California's pervasive reservoirs had become prime fishing waters. To meet this demand, the state built more hatcheries and raised more fish. It started planting "catchable-sized" trout, e.g. eight to ten inches, for the instant gratification of anglers, that is, "put-and-take" fishing.

Today, bodies of water up and down California hold a variety of both native and introduced game fish. None hold more than Shasta Lake, where fifteen species exist, many a result of annual stockings: Chinook salmon, rainbow trout, brown trout, largemouth bass, smallmouth bass, spotted bass, black bullhead, brown bullhead, white catfish, channel catfish, green sunfish, bluegill, black crappie, white crappie, and white sturgeon. Shasta Lake has become one of the most outstanding still waters for fishing in California.

~

The transformation of California's waterways was thorough. Reservoirs now dominate the Golden State, their waters carried to distant places to turn landscapes green where they used to be tan, and modest communities into huge metropolises. These impoundments—home to native and many non-native fish—also offer endless angling adventures.

As the state's largest and most important waterway, the Sacramento River provided the greatest impetus for these changes. Groups and governments radically altered the river, triggering consequences not readily apparent or conveniently ignored. Before the twentieth century ended, however, attention to these far-reaching repercussions had become the primary agenda in going forward.

Angler with his catch of a spotted bass, an introduced game fish at Shasta Lake. John Gantner.

Delta sunset, Mt. Diablo in the distance. Bobby Barrack.

CHAPTER SIX

Decline of the Delta

"Everything in nature is attracted to estuaries and rich coastlines."

—*John Flicker, The Audubon Society*

Estuaries are among the richest and most complex and richest environments on the planet. They connect mountains with oceans. They provide a transition zone between salt and fresh water, and for the creatures able to live in each. An estuary's waters and elements blend in a ballet of circulation patterns to create a nutrient-packed environment far richer than anything humans could ever create.

At one time the estuary now known as the Sacramento–San Joaquin Delta was a great biological engine that birthed one of the world's richest food webs. The region intricately linked thousands of multi-braided channels and hundreds of islands; dense forests; more than a half-million acres of tidal marshes and wetlands; peat soils so organically rich they could ignite; insects by the trillions; fish species migrating from sea to mountain streams and back; thousands of marine species; an avian paradise; iconic animals such as grizzly bears and tule elk; and mineral-laden waters that created, nourished, and cleansed as they ebbed and flowed.

The two largest California rivers forming the Delta drained the Cascade Mountains and coastal ranges, and the western Sierra Nevada to its southernmost boundaries. They carried their liquid bounties to this estuary and eventually the sea. Along the way they gathered and deposited organic plant and animal matter, creating vibrantly fertile top soils. Material deposited in the broad alluvial fan—the actual Delta formation—constituted the most productive part of this precious substance. Residue from decaying giant bulrushes—called tules—added to the mix, along with other tidal wetland vegetation. The resulting composition, known as humus, or peat, was as deep as fifty feet in places.

With the exception of water, few substances are as important to a healthy planet as rich, hardy earth. Intrinsically more valuable than precious metals, soil creates and supports life. Delta soil was especially replete with organisms of all kinds, which feasted on the detritus deposited from sources both far and close.

When the rivers flooded and stormed out to the sea, outflows flushed these elements into the Pacific Ocean, where they refurbished the sea and its creatures. This included the most storied of all, salmon, which absorbed these nutrients and returned them inland during their migrations.

What lived in the water itself further en-

"Dawn Kiss." Sandhill cranes engaging in mating ritual. Lon Yarbrough.

dowed the Delta with unparalleled fertility. Foremost was the microscopic phytoplankton, which inhabits the upper sunlit layers of most water bodies and stimulates photosynthesis and oxygenation. Their animal equivalent is zooplankton. Both are critical to estuaries, where they move with the tides, infuse sediment, and sustain aquatic life.

Residents of the Delta include the ancient sturgeon, whose continued existence depends on the rich brackish waters. While they may cruise coastal waters and swim to upper reaches of the river, these fish need the Delta to survive. Other resident fish belong to the smelt family, including the delta smelt, longfin smelt, and an anadromous species—the eulachon. The Delta is also where salmon prepare to go from salt water to fresh water, or with juveniles from fresh water to salt water—each a critical phase in their life histories.

At one time, sturgeon and smelt and salmon all flourished, along with grizzly bears, tule elk, sandhill cranes, and tundra swans, in concert with the Delta's unique rhythms. But human intrusions eventually shattered this complex, intricate mosaic of water and land and its interlocking chain of organisms.

A white sturgeon. Joe Ferreira.

Remaking the Delta

When governmental authorities scanned the Delta in the mid-1880s, they saw "worthless swamplands" in need of reclamation. The priority to create useable land in the region persisted far into the twentieth century

Major reclamation projects in the Delta began in 1861 when the federal government transferred ownership of Delta lands to the State of California. By 1871, most of the lands had been sold to private owners, with the state using the income to reclaim the lands, primarily by constructing levees that would allow land to dry and become productive.

Chinese laborers constructed many of the initial levees—work which involved scooping out soil and piling it up to make dirt walls. Such hand labor eventually proved inadequate for this enormous undertaking. Steam-powered dredges that excavated large volumes of soil from river channels were brought in. These were followed by even larger clamshell-type dredges. By the 1920s, nearly all of the marshland had been reclaimed, leading to far fewer channels and islands. More than eleven hundred miles of levees, still largely in place today, protected the drained lands. Most of this acreage is devoted

Clamshell dredger at work in the Delta. Courtesy of Rio Vista Museum.

to crops such as pears, corn, grain, sugar beets, tomatoes, and especially asparagus.

From the outset, the remaking of the Delta was rife with problems. The very richness and multi-character of the peat soil made it unstable. Exposed to air, the dirt was subject to oxygenation that decomposed it and released carbon dioxide. In the process it shrank and compacted. The protected lands began subsiding at the rate of one to three inches a year. The islands, rather than prominent features, became sunken depressions.

Further, as the peat dried, winds picked up the fine sediment and sent it skyward, creating dark "peat

Levees protecting Delta farmlands. Bureau of Reclamation.

storms" that drifted over Stockton. Deep cracks and fissures developed. Farmers patched up cracks by piling on more dirt.

As land sank, levees got higher, putting even greater pressure on them. Levee failures were common—almost two hundred times over the past century—flooding islands and farm lands. For instance, on a sunny day in 2004, the levee

and earthquakes surely will lead to rising water and more levee failures. Some liken this potential calamity to what happened to the Gulf Coast when Hurricane Katrina hit. Should it occur, and it most likely will without preventive action, the resultant flooding would threaten lives, property, and drinking water supplies. To head off catastrophe, the Department of Water

The collapse of this levee caused massive Delta flooding. Bureau of Reclamation.

protecting one tract collapsed without warning. The freed water covered the island's asparagus and tomato farms up to twelve feet. It took more than six months to pump out the water.

Delta reclamation reduced natural wetlands to a few thousand acres, generally in small isolated patches. To facilitate auto travel, more than fifty bridges were built to span what channels remained. The reclaimed lands, including at least half of the islands, settled ten to twenty feet below sea level, protected only by precarious levees, most never built to meet structural standards. They are part of the fourteen thousand built in California during the past 150 years, a piecemeal flood-control system based on antiquated technologies. Climate change

Resources in 2011 issued a plan to repair and upgrade the entire system at a cost of between $14 billion and $17 billion.

Beyond these physical alterations to the Delta, changes to its water created a different set of problems.

In order to transfer water from the north state to the arid San Joaquin Valley and urban south, the Delta became the "vast switching yard." First the Central Valley Project created a massive pumping station south of the Delta near the town of Tracy. Six pumps take Delta water and send it to farms in the San Joaquin Valley. The State Water Project followed with more pumps that shunt Delta water to the 444-mile-long California Aqueduct and other conveyances that supply mainly residential users, from the Bay Area to San Diego. Almost two-thirds of Californians, more than twenty million people, get at least part of their drinking water from the Delta.

The federal and state water projects have taken as much as forty percent of the Delta's water—an amount that could flood one thou-

and Sacramento perch, or threatened with extinction. The latter includes Central Valley steelhead and green sturgeon. White sturgeon have declined to a fifty-year low of about ten thousand fish. Chinook salmon runs have seen devastating drops.

And in what many see as the starkest indicator of the Delta's possible collapse, delta smelt

Delta farmland inundated by flood. Bureau of Reclamation.

sand football fields more than a mile deep. This is all water that used to keep the estuary functioning as it did for millennia.

Indicators of Collapse

The Delta's makeover had deep repercussions. By the time they became fully apparent and commitments were launched to protect what remained, much of the damage had already occurred.

The most documentable are alarming declines in phytoplankton and zooplankton—foundations of the estuary's web of life. Another is the crisis in fish populations. Twenty-nine known fish species once called the Delta home. Twelve are either gone, like the thicktail chub

numbers have plunged, despite its being listed as a threatened species under state and federal laws in the 1990s. Longfin smelt and threadfin shad are also now a small fraction of their historic populations.

As these native species were crashing, invasive exotic species were coming to dominate most of the Delta's waters.

While past populations of delta smelt are unknown, sampling procedures show a drop of almost ninety-eight percent in their numbers since the early 1990s. The fish could become extinct in less than twenty years. This precipitous decline reveals that the delicate lifestyle of this fish and its habitat are no longer in sync. With less water in the Delta, out-

Delta Smelt

THE UNDERWATER world of the Delta was once one of the most dynamic and textured of aquatic settings. A medley of constantly changing currents caressed flora and fauna to foster a harmonious blending, from the microscopic to the giant. Millions of small fish swam in montages of mysterious choreography. This was the world of the delta smelt.

Delta smelt are a translucent fish about two and one-half inches long with a steel-blue lateral stripe and the pleasant aroma of cucumber. They are found only in the Bay-Delta estuary and spend their entire lives there, making them highly sensitive to environmental changes in the region. Their rhythms and those of the Delta are as synchronized as partners in a dance.

When it's time to spawn, salty tidal currents carry delta smelt from the brackish waters of the Upper Suisun Bay back into the estuary. The fish then swim to its upper parts to lay their eggs in freshwater side channels and sloughs. After spawning, almost all adults die. The eggs remain attached to submerged aquatic vegetation. After hatching, the newborn fish drift down the estuary to the Delta's mouth and upper bay, where fresh water and salt water mix in what is called the entrapment zone. There the currents keep the larvae in suspension, while they feed on zooplankton. When the dry season returns and incoming tidal currents are able once again to push farther up the estuary due to weaker freshwater flows, the cycle is renewed.

A delta smelt, barometer of Delta health. Bureau of Reclamation.

Boat docked at Rio Vista, a Delta town of many charms. Bureau of Reclamation.

flows are reduced or abruptly increased from pumping regimens. Such unnatural flows disrupt the tenuous balance between fish and currents. Pumps also suck in and grind up fish; toxins harm them; and exotic species prey on the smelt or deplete the zooplankton that smelt rely on for food. These factors also impact other native species. Delta smelt are a vital source of food for larger fish, like young salmon on their downriver migrations, and myriad birds. The loss of this forage fish affects the well-being of many other fish, birds, and animals.

Scientists believe there are three major causes for the potential ecological collapse of the Delta: water diversions; poor water quality; and the introduction and spread of invasive species. Each of these factors presents a minefield of contending groups and values.

First, depletion of water.

Water Diversions

Because so many entities and organisms depend on water, it is the most controversial of all issues. Politics weigh heavily in this arena. Typically, environmental and fishing organizations line up against corporate farms. Needs of growing urban areas are also involved. The stakes could not be higher.

On one side is a natural environment and some of California's most valued native species heading toward probable collapse and extinction. On the other is the country's most productive food-producing region. Agribusinesses and its arch supporters argue that people's needs are more important than fish, an argument that ignores those whose livelihoods depend on fish, particularly salmon. All these stakeholders are dependent on the Delta's water.

Laws such as the Endangered Species Act

(ESA) and Clean Water Act protect native species and water quality. Some politicians who support farmers have tried to overturn the ESA or its designations since it is the primary tool for protecting native species like delta smelt. Lawsuits are standard to seek resolution, and the courts often make these critical decisions.

At issue is the degree to which water diversions are responsible for the Delta's decline.

The National Resources Defense Council (NRDC) studied data in five-year intervals across five decades of water diversions from the Delta by federal and state water projects. The results showed that the downward trajectory of the Delta as indicated by species decline coincided with a steady increase in the quantity of diverted water. Kate Poole, lead attorney on the case for the NRDC, stated, "We're watching our salmon disappear in exact concert with a 16 percent increase of delta water diversions over the last decade."

Beyond losses of fresh water, pumping stations suck in and grind up juvenile salmon and steelhead as they attempt to migrate though the Delta to the ocean. The toll on all fish species besides salmon and steelhead—including splittail, threadfin shad, American shad, and striped bass—from such "salvaging" in any given year totals almost twelve million. The pumping also alters the natural flow regimes of the Delta, which in turn disrupts fish behaviors. And it sucks water with such force it reverses the flow of two small waterways, the Old and the Middle rivers, which now flow backward.

Diversions increase the salinity of the Delta, as the remaining fresh water often isn't sufficient to dilute the salt carried by ocean water flowing in from San Francisco Bay. The higher concentration of saline water harms both the fishery and crop production and generates common concern.

In 2004, the Bush administration significantly increased water exports from the Delta to Central Valley farmers. It also took other agricultural-friendly actions, such as relaxing cold-water flow requirements and removing the Sacramento splittail from the Endangered Species Act—despite consensus by scientists that it needed such protection. Stripping an endangered species of its designation means loss of habitat protections, which in this case freed up more water for farmers.

As native fisheries continued to decline, a coalition of fishermen, conservation, and Native American groups, including the Sacramento River Preservation Trust, Earthjustice, National Resources Defense Council, Pacific Coast Federation of Fishermen's Association, and The Bay Institute, filed a lawsuit in 2005. It claimed that these changes reversed protections credited with saving endangered winter-run salmon from extinction.

On April 16, 2008, U.S. District Judge Oliver W. Wanger ruled that the federal government's biological opinion approving operation of the state and federal water projects violated the Endangered Species Act. The judge relied on the federal National Marine Fisheries Service's (NMFS) own finding that the current operations of the projects "…result in the loss of 42 percent of the juvenile winter-run Chinook population, and proposed project effects are expected to result in an additional 3 to 20 percent loss of the juvenile population."

NMFS also found that the plan to export more water from the Delta would kill up to 66 percent of Central Valley steelhead and 57 percent of juvenile spring-run Chinook salmon, and would likely lead to their extinction . The court ruled the federal government's finding that the projects would not jeopardize listed salmonid species simply didn't square with the facts.

In July 2008, Judge Wanger reaffirmed his earlier ruling and explicitly held that current water operations are jeopardizing the existence of the three species—winter-run Chinook salmon, Central Valley spring-run Chinook salmon, and Central Valley steelhead—and must be modified to protect them. The ruling also found that current water operations threaten killer whales, which rely on Sacramento River salmon as a major food source.

The court opinion established a new set of rules under which the state and federal water projects must operate to protect California's imperiled salmon. Key measures in the new biological opinion include:

❡ Requiring more cold water held behind Shasta Dam for release during salmon migration and spawning seasons.

❡ Modifying operation of Delta Cross Channel Gates to reduce the number of juvenile salmon unnaturally pushed to their deaths by predation and Delta water pumps.

❡ Requiring better flows and colder water to enhance salmon spawning and habitat in the American and Stanislaus rivers.

❡ Reducing water pumping when juvenile salmon migrate through the Delta.

In applauding the decision, George Torgun of Earthjustice said, "The Bush-era plan for water operations in California was not based in science and it devastated coastal fishing communities throughout California as the salmon population plummeted. This biological opinion brings back some needed balance. Now fishing communities, native California salmon species, and water users will all operate on a level playing field."

Water Quality

The Delta's waters suffer from contaminants, primarily from agriculture. Farms apply more than 200 million pounds of pesticide every year. These pathogens, nitrates, and salts enter Central Valley rivers and streams and ultimately end up in the Delta, where they devastate aquatic habitat, contribute to the collapse of fisheries and other wildlife, and threaten drinking water. Yet such agricultural runoff has been exempt from the federal Clean Water Act. California's clean water law does require regulations if agricultural pollution is shown to harm the environment, but the State Water Board has not imposed strong and permanent controls on water quality.

The watchdog agency for pollution in the San Francisco Bay and Delta is Baykeeper, which seeks to strengthen clean water laws and hold polluters accountable. In 2007, Baykeeper filed suit against the Central Valley Regional Water Quality Control Board for allowing agribusinesses to freely pollute public waterways. Joined by the California Sportfishing Protection Alliance, Baykeeper requested that the decision not to hold agriculture responsible for pollution be overturned. But the State Water Board allowed the waivers to stand. Baykeeper has challenged this illegal loophole in court, and continues to argue that regulations over agricultural runoff should be implemented and enforced.

Other waterway pollutants include common household pesticides, runoff from treated lawns, liquid drippings from cars, toxins from paints, and chlorine from swimming pools. The American River, for example, flows thirty miles through a highly urbanized area from which it receives an influx of toxins. Adding to this infusion is the discharge of treated sewage into the Sacramento River by the Sacramento Regional Wastewater Treatment Plant. Such sewage discharges, not only in the Sacramento area but elsewhere, contain toxic contaminants such as ammonia, heavy metals, and pharmaceuticals. These chemicals wind up in the Delta, where they kill organisms such as the tiny shrimp (*Hyalella azteca*), another vital link in the Delta's food chain.

As contaminants kill more native species, harmful invasive ones take their place.

Exotic Species

At least 250 exotic species from distant continents live in the San Francisco Bay estuary and Delta. They get introduced in many ways: from ships (and their cargo) traveling up the deep water channels to Stockton and Sacramento; on materials like rocks and wood used as ballast on vessels; from recreational and commercial boats; from the disposal of aquarium and water-garden materials; from fishing bait; through new foods and other commercial products that find their way into waters; through deliberate introduction, often mischievous in nature; and from wanton dumping. In their new homes, exotic species often proliferate and wreak havoc, pushing out native species like mollusks, crustaceans, hydroids, bryozoans, and aquatic grasses.

For example, a small mollusk called the Asian or "overbite" clam—*Corbula amurensis*—has displaced all other invertebrates in tens of thousands of acres in the bay estuary, reducing biological diversity to almost zero. Before the clam showed up in the 1980s, large portions of the bay supported extravagant phytoplankton blooms and huge populations of zooplankton, buttressing a vast aquatic food web that ranged from tiny fish and crustraceans to big halibut and leopard sharks. The introduced clams are voracious consumers of both phytoplankton and zooplankton, and are so numerous in places—reaching densities of fifty thousand per square meter—that they suck up all the plankton and create a totally new mono-environment.

Another exotic is the Chinese mitten crab, which can wreck biological communities through predation and competition. Commer-

Chinese mitten crab, an exotic species wreaking damage on the Delta's ecoysystem. Bureau of Reclamation.

Choking of a slough by the exotic water primrose plant. Gregg Werner.

cial shrimpers first collected this invasive species in South San Francisco Bay in 1993. Authorities suspect it was deliberately introduced as a possible food source. These foreign crabs, which are able to walk over land, invaded other waters. By 1998 mitten crabs had populated not only the bay, but well up the Sacramento River system, where they prey on salmonid and sturgeon eggs and juveniles, and destroy the aquatic food chain. Mitten crabs also burrow into banks during low tides, causing bank erosion and weakened levees.

Exotic plants, too, can be highly destructive. One, the colorful water hyacinth, doubles in size every ten days and is taking over large swaths of the Delta. A South American native imported in the early 1990s, it chokes waterways, reduces oxygen levels, and increases silt and organic matter. Other exotic species like hydrilla and sparline are also growing rampant in the waterways. All of this threatens fish and the Delta itself.

A more complicated picture is presented by introduced fish. As already noted, sunfish have caused the extirpation of the native Sacra-

mento perch from most of its original waters. But introduced species like the largemouth bass and striped bass have proven to be outstanding sport fish for anglers, and in the case of the latter, highly valued for their tasty flesh. Yet such predatory species may be impacting salmon—the subject for the next chapter.

~

No one has been able to state definitively why the Delta is crashing. Or if there is a single most compelling reason, which, if addressed, could turn the dismal picture around and begin the Delta's long journey back to health. The assaults on this vital network of water are deeply rooted, widespread, and unrelenting. What we do know is that the present course is unsustainable and growing more consequential with each passing year.

In July of 2010 the State Water Resources Control Board and the California Environmental Protection Agency issued a critical report—*Development of Flow Criteria for the Sacramento-San Joaquin Delta Ecosystem.* Its findings and conclusions state the issues as follows (digested from the original summary):

1. The performance of native and desirable fish populations in the Delta requires much more than freshwater flows. While folks ask, "How much water do fish need?" they might well also ask, "How much habitat of different types and locations, suitable water quality, improved food supply and fewer invasive species that is maintained by better governance institutions, competent implementation and directed research do fish need?" The answers to these questions are interdependent. We do know that current policies have been disastrous for desirable fish. It took over a century to change the Delta's ecosystem to a less desirable state; it will take many decades to put it back together again with a different physical, biological, economic, and institutional environment.

Gates regulating amounts of saline water that enter the Delta. Bureau of Reclamation.

2. Recent Delta flows are insufficient to support native Delta fishes for today's habitats.

3. Restoring environmental variability in the Delta is fundamentally inconsistent with continuing to move large volumes of water through the Delta for export. The drinking and agricultural water quality requirements of through-Delta exports, and perhaps even some current in-Delta uses, are at odds with the water quality and variability of desirable Delta species.

4. The Delta ecosystem is likely to dramatically shift within fifty years due to large-scale levee collapse. Overall, these changes are likely to promote a more variable, heterogeneous estuary. This changed environment is likely to be better for desirable estuarine species; at least it is unlikely to be worse.

5. Positive changes in the Delta ecosystem resulting from improved flow or flow patterns will benefit humans as well as fish and wildlife.

6. Ecosystems are complex; many factors affect the quality of the habitat that they provide. The habitat value of the Delta ecosystem for favorable species can be improved by habitat restoration, contaminant and nutrient reduction, changes in diversions, control of invasive species, and island flooding.

7. The State Water Board supports the most efficient use of water that can reasonably be made. The flow improvements that the State Water Board identifies in this report as being necessary to protect public trust resources illustrate the importance of addressing the negative effects of these other stressors that contribute to higher than necessary demands for water to provide resource protection.

Restore the Delta

RESTORE THE DELTA is a broad coalition of citizens and organizations that has formed to strengthen the estuary's health and well-being of Delta communities. To accomplish this, Restore the Delta has initiated a campaign to reduce water exports. This will help restore the Delta's ecosystem; protect native and other desirable species; maintain public health; ensure that water quality meets federal and state water standards; enable fisheries and farming to thrive as they have historically; and protect the region's economic interests.

Barbara Barrigan-Parrilla, campaign director of Restore the Delta, states: "Whether one fishes or farms the Delta, spends her weekends boating up and down its waterways, bird watches, attends the region's numerous farming and cultural festivals, drinks white or red wine from Delta wineries, drives trucks full of Delta produce, sells insurance to Delta marinas and farms, drinks municipal water from the Delta—the Delta is our home. Our present and future environmental and economic well-being is tied to the health of this estuary. All that we value in terms of work, quality of life, and recreation is dependent upon the quality and quantity of water passing through the Delta. Fighting to protect the Delta is about people and the deep value of a region that has been misused by outsiders, and sometimes not fully appreciated or protected by its own people. It's about believing in something bigger and better than just the desires of individual stakeholders.

"Delta defenders, local water agency leaders, engineers, fishing leaders, engaged business people and politicos, and involved California environmentalists and Delta farmers live their love for this region through their ongoing advocacy and vigilance on behalf of the estuary."

Chinook salmon. Doug Killam.

CHAPTER SEVEN

Decline of Salmon

"A god lives deep in the ocean—the Great God Salmon. Once a year this spirit offers a sacrifice to humans by putting on salmon skin and returning to the land. When the first salmon show up in the spring, a single fish is taken to an altar. There the inner spirit is thanked for returning. If offended, the salmon will not return."

—Native American legend

To have Chinook salmon in a river is to have life rapturously expressed in the briefest of snapshots. One will often unleash bursts of energy, spontaneously leaping out of the water and then crashing back down on its side or back, as though celebrating its last days with spurts of remaining force. How else to explain the launching of cartwheels, first one, then another, and another, and yet one more, as the fish explodes from the current in a dazzling display of jumps and somersaults.

Chinook salmon are also called "king," a name well deserved. A specimen can grow to five feet and weigh 125 pounds. It is one of America's true wilderness icons, along with the bison, grizzly bear, cougar, golden eagle, and elk. Beyond its sacred place in waterways, the salmon's flesh is treasured as a culinary delicacy, which adds both to its appeal and its threatened status.

The story of salmon mirrors the saga of the American West, where efforts to transform arid regions into gardens and metropolises unwit-

tingly caused the demise of the creature which, more than any other, bestowed magnificence wherever it chose to go.

When Salmon Return

Chinook salmon spend the majority of their brief life in the ocean, usually three to four years. In this nutrient-rich environment, they grow hefty and strong, their bodies gathering nitrogen, phosphorous, carbon, and other essential elements. When they leave the sea to spawn, they somehow follow an internal geo-magnetic compass, aided by visual cues and distinctive odors, to return unerringly to their birthplace waterways, their fat-laden, powerful bodies a veritable storehouse of energy, protein, and minerals. In migration, Chinook possess one purpose—to propagate.

Approaching their destinations, their silvery blue color gradually darkens. Once at a spawning site where flowing water and gravel are available, the female uses her tail to excavate a shallow depression or spawning bed, called a redd

Two generations of Chinook salmon. Doug Killam.

Dead salmon, its life's mission completed. Bob Madgic.

Bald eagles consuming salmon carcass. Bob Madgic.

All that remains of a fish whose flesh fed many organisms. Bob Madgic.

(from the Scottish phrase "to make ready"). She then deposits as many as five thousand eggs. A nearby male salmon quickly fertilizes the eggs by releasing streams of sperm, enriching the aqua-environment in the process. The female disturbs the gravel at the upstream edge of the depression to cover the eggs, then goes to a different location to make another redd. Before

lay eggs in carcasses, spurring hatches, which provide more food for fish and birds. One study showed as many as 139 animal species benefiting from salmon remains.

Before long only the skeleton remains. But the ocean nutrients the salmon carried will often be spread far and wide. Nitrogen of marine origin might show up in the hair of bears. A

The next generation—a salmon alevin. Doug Killam.

her supply of eggs is exhausted, the female may make as many as seven redds. Both salmon parents remain nearby to ward off predators.

As the salmon linger, their bodies begin to deteriorate. They start drifting listlessly, and their skin becomes mottled. They lose their ability to swim upright, turning instead onto their sides, then onto their backs. Within two weeks from the time they deposit and fertilize the eggs, the salmon will die, their purpose fulfilled.

Carcasses accumulate in the river and along the shores. Bacteria and fungi abet the decaying process, giving the waterway a distinct aroma. But even in death salmon sustain life. Scavenging birds and mammals consume the flesh; bugs and maggots join the feast. Insects

bald eagle may have ripped off fragments of skin and flesh and deposited leftovers far away. Scat of animals and birds that consumed salmon will be full of nutrients and bones, which fertilize riparian vegetation and nourish forests. Agricultural crops in fields near salmon rivers have been enriched from marine-derived nutrients. In some California vineyards, compounds traceable to salmon were found in zinfandel grapes!

After the parents have died, the eggs remain in the redds for up to four weeks. A number routinely spill out, providing fish such as trout and steelhead with protein to consume. In due time, a tiny fish-like creature—an alevin— emerges from an egg, an attached yolk sac its sole food source. It can't swim. Vulnerable to predators, the alevin hides under gravel to avoid being eaten.

When an alevin finally absorbs its yolk sac, it is a tiny fish about an inch long—the fry stage. Fry typically dwell in the vicinity of the redd for several months, feeding on their parents' remains and nearby insects. By the time a fry heads downstream, it is a parr—or fingerling—about two inches long. A gauntlet of peril awaits as it proceeds slowly downriver, often taking many months to reach the ocean. More than ninety percent do not make it due mainly to predators, including fish and birds like egrets, herons, and kingfishers. As with their parents, young salmon provide food for other river organisms.

If a salmon makes it to the estuary, it's usually more than a year old and over five inches long—the smolt stage. It remains in this brackish "nursery" for more than half a year, feeding and growing, while its body chemistry adjusts to the salty water. When it enters the ocean it is an adult fish. The cycle is then repeated. (Note: the timelines and locations presented above may vary considerably, depending on the particular life cycle of a fish. More on these variations will follow.)

How Salmon Came to Be

It is believed salmon originated in fresh water. Their earliest ancestors were a new type of fish called teleosts—fishes whose skeletons were made of cartilage rather than bone, and which came to populate lakes and streams of western North America. Fossil records show the first known salmonid ancestor looked like today's grayling. Along with ancient trout and whitefishes—which still exist today—it lived in primeval lakes in western Canada approximately forty to fifty million years ago. It seems likely, therefore, that the first salmon also lived in inland lakes and rivers as its forebears did. But this species evolved to live in both fresh and salt water, a remarkable life strategy that led to their ecological dominance along the coasts of North America and beyond.

It probably happened this way: Tens of millions of years ago, violent periods of volcanoes and earthquakes blocked and rechanneled rivers, forming large inland lakes. Evaporation led to increased alkalinity (similar to California's Eagle and Mono lakes). As generations of salmonid bred in these isolated lakes, fish best able to withstand wide fluctuations in salinity and temperature survived and spawned offspring with the same hardiness.

Being able to survive in both fresh and saline water gave salmon increased range and flexibility. In time they migrated from inland lakes and streams to food-rich waters of the Pacific Ocean. But to spawn the next generation, instinct drove them to return to the waters of their birth. Their robust size and strength enabled them to swim farther into the continent and produce more offspring than resident salmonid.

Salmon kept adapting. When ice ages descended on the northern regions of Alaska and the Yukon, salmon traveled south to ice-free rivers in Oregon and California. After the ice retreated, salmon returned again to northern waters, the region now a moonlike landscape of rock and glacial wash. Whatever fry hatched in this exposed environment had to survive scorching suns and hungry birds. Lack of vegetation and forests meant few insects.

Gradually the climate became more temperate, resulting in a cool, wet maritime pattern that enabled forests to grow. Over time, old-growth stands of trees encased and shaded streams, with downed snags in river channels creating pools and side channels. Salmon thrived once again, bringing life-enriching nutrients from the ocean to wherever they journeyed.

The Salmon's World

Up and down the Northwest, salmon swam to distant inland regions, fighting their way up rapids, cascades, shoots, and falls that only the strongest and most tenacious of fish could eclipse. (The word "salmon" is taken from the Latin word *salir*—to leap.) Only a large waterfall or other impassable obstruction could stop them. In the Columbia River Basin—the largest river system in the West and once home to the biggest Chinook run in the world—no such blockages existed on the main river and its major tributary, the Snake, so fish traveled over a thousand miles up these rivers, into British Columbia and Idaho, where the Salmon River and its tributaries produced forty-five percent of all salmon in the system.

In California, they swam up the Klamath River, on into Oregon. Many left the Klamath to go up its largest tributary, the crystal-clear Trinity River. The majority of runs occurred in the Sacramento system, encompassing the Sacramento, McCloud, Pit, Feather, Yuba, and American rivers and their many tributaries. Fish used every waterway, no matter how small, as sheer numbers required ever-new spawning niches.

The southernmost river for salmon migrations was the Ventura River in Southern California. But it was the vast San Joaquin system, including tributaries like the Merced, Stanislaus, Calaveras, Tuolumne, Mokelumne, and Consumnes, that rivaled Sacramento's for salmon abundance. Most of these rivers originated in the high Sierra Nevada, where plentiful stores of clear, cold water gushed down mountainsides to the foothills, attracting salmon and steelhead in droves. Some salmon entered the river in the spring and held over the summer in cold, deep pools fed by vast reserves of snowmelt. When rains arrived in the fall and the streams swelled, these Chinook literally swam up mountains to spawn in the gravels and rocky cobbles of high-elevation streams.

This was the salmon's ecosystem: the long chain of marine, estuarine, and freshwater habitats that fish navigated to complete their anadromous life cycles.

In their migrations, individual salmon follow inner timetables and use varied waters to fit their tastes. One class of salmon—referred to as "stream-type Chinook"—remains many months in fresh water. Their offspring likewise stay long, usually over a year. A second grouping spends far less time in fresh water, usually spawning in lower parts of a river. Their progeny also don't linger very long and return quickly to sea, where these "ocean-type Chinook" gain most of their first-year growth.

As this saga developed, variations ruled, exceptions determining strength. Unique subspecies—"races"—evolved, genetically distinct "runs" programmed to migrate and spawn the same time year after year, using assorted waters throughout river basins—from small tributary streams to slow sections of large rivers—to carve out their life niches. In the Sacramento system, four Chinook runs developed—spring-run, fall-run, late-fall-run, and winter-run—each adapted to different times of the year, parts of the river system, and differing conditions. While one race of Chinook was migrating back to the ocean, another was moving upriver. Every month of the year saw spawning salmon.

In all cases, the estuary phase of their life's journey is critical. It is where salmon prepare to go from salt water to fresh water—or with juveniles, from fresh water to salt water. In this stage, too, distinctions predominated, with estuarine residency ranging from a few weeks to many months.

This kind of diversification or variability—"multiple life strategies"—increased the traits and number of fish capable of breeding in the same waterways year after year. It rewarded adaptation, built resilience, and perpetuated genetic distinctiveness, all critical for species survival. Changing conditions, disease, and other catastrophes test the ability of a community to survive. The more complex a species is, the more likely it will survive. The world of salmon has always been complex.

Salmon thus adapted to whatever they encountered in nature, however extreme. What is not clear is whether they can survive alongside humankind.

Salmon under Siege

Author Timothy Egan writes: "The Pacific Northwest is simply this: wherever the salmon can get to. From the Sacramento to the Yukon, every waterway pulled by gravity to the Pacific has, at one time, been full of the silver flash of life." This is no longer the case. With each development phase of the West, salmon—the very essence of the Northwest—kept losing.

Of all the causes behind salmon declines, dams have been the most harmful. Waterscapes were radically reconfigured in favor of "cheap power" and water for agriculture and industry. Construction of numerous dams blocked salmon migration on just about all waterways throughout the Northwest. (One example is the Snake River, where fifteen dams have reduced this once muscular and bountiful river to a string of lakes.) Dams also blocked gravel and sediment—which fish need for spawning—from being dispersed throughout the river. (Ironically, every reservoir eventually will be filled with sediment, rendering it useless, the accumulated silt a huge residual problem.) Dams capture and warm a river's water, and produce unnatural flow regimes.

With dams in place, salmon have to swim up artificial fish ladders or be trucked or barged so they can continue upriver. Huge numbers die at dams and in the warmer reservoirs below. Returning juvenile fish are bused around these dams and other migratory obstacles to facilitate their trip to the ocean. Such artificial maneuvers—"migratory pinball"—chiseled away at the biological maps of salmon and created large missing pieces in their migration puzzles. They shattered the salmon's ecosystem and evolutionary trajectory. The foundations for a collapse of the fishery had been established, and that's exactly what happened.

Many factors figured in the demise of salmon beyond this piecemeal destruction of their natural universe. Rivers were rip rapped and channelized, altering natural features upon which fish depended. Ruinous mining practices and erosive logging operations clogged and contaminated waterways; riparian forests were heedlessly cut down, further degrading waterways. Water diversions to distant farms and cities deprived rivers and estuaries of their full supply.

In addition, huge numbers of salmon were caught and sold for food. Salmon canneries up and down the Northwest ushered in a multi-million-dollar industry. The first cannery on the Sacramento River opened in 1864; by the 1880s, nineteen canneries produced two hundred thousand cases of salmon annually.

Along with this commercialization, fish managers pursued strategies geared more for renewable commodities than wild creatures. In hatcheries that sprouted seemingly everywhere as mitigation for dams, biologists (many hired by canneries) often selected salmon spawning partners, controlled rearing conditions, dictated the sizes, times, and locations for releasing fish, and regulated harvest levels to achieve maximum yield. In short, wild fish became more domesticated through an agricultural production model based on efficiency and standardization.

As salmon runs kept plummeting, officials clung to the belief that technology could fix matters, and hatchery production could compensate for any losses.

But the declining numbers of returning salmon reflected this abuse and these mistruths. *The fish had been offended.*

Salmon and the Sacramento River

When construction of Shasta Dam began in 1938, authorities had to know that salmon runs would be adversely affected. The dam would permanently block fish from approximately fifty percent of their spawning and rearing habitat in the river and upper watershed. Water releases would create higher flows in the summer to supply water for agriculture. This runs counter to the instinctual behaviors of salmon.

But other priorities ruled, like water storage and delivery to the Central Valley, flood control, and energy production. Fish technocrats were left to figure out what to do about salmon. In the words of author Michael Black, what followed was "a set of serialistic policies—a succession of pure technological solutions to mitigate against collapsing fisheries, all seeking a triumph of the artificial." He referred to these as "tragic remedies."

The first "solution" came in 1942 when the federal government established the primary piece in a "Shasta Salvage Plan"—Coleman National Fish Hatchery on Battle Creek in Anderson. There, officials annually collect and hatch salmon eggs, then raise fry to a sufficient size for a percentage of them to make it to the ocean and return as mature fish. (Such fish are "hatchery stock," in contrast to "wild fish" born and raised in the river, some of which also go to Coleman.) The original goal was to collect fifty million eggs, but in most years this number settles at twenty million.

Not all salmon return to Coleman, of course. The (Sacramento-only) winter-run that had migrated up the Upper Sacramento, McCloud, and Pit rivers still seek to go there. They continue upriver past Battle Creek, only to be stopped by Keswick Dam, where authorities capture them at the dam's base—the "Keswick trap." They are then taxied to the Livingston Stone National Fish Hatchery at Shasta Dam's base, where fish eggs are hatched and fry raised. These are taken by truck and released back into the Sacramento. Such deprivation of their historic waters and natural spawning behaviors have severely compromised this race of salmon.

In the 1960s, another major blow was delivered. Right where the Sacramento began turning colder and some fish typically started to spawn, the U.S. Bureau of Reclamation constructed a river-spanning "diversion dam" to provide water to farmers via canals—the Corning and Tehama–Colusa canals. When the gates were down—about two and one-half months a year—this "Red Bluff Diversion Dam" impeded fish migrations, while creating a seasonal lake that inundated six miles of prime gravel beds that annually produced about 6,000 salmon. (The lake soon was providing speed-boating recreation and economic returns for the city of Red Bluff.) To replace the natural spawning beds, two rock-lined channels, each two miles long, were constructed alongside the dam for salmon to spawn. Officials called this plan a "fish enhancer" that would produce 23,000 fish.

The spawning channels did not produce one mature salmon. The problem, according to Bill Kier, former DFG official and fisheries consultant, was that "salmon don't like to spawn in gravel-lined concrete ditches with no bankside vegetation. They want natural riffles cooled by heavy forest growth. They need channels with irregular banks where the baby salmon can escape from predators." According to Kier, "a

The now defunct Red Bluff Diversion Dam, with reconstructed pumping plant, fish screen, and canals. Bureau of Reclamation.

positive spin had to be put on any project of the Bureau of Reclamation, and the idea promoted that technological fixes can improve on nature. Projects like this one pretty much discredit that philosophy."

Fish ladders were also placed on either side of the dam to provide fish passage. But salmon were drawn to the strong and impassable flows of the main spillway, not the weak flows of the ladders. The fish milled helplessly in front of the dam face, or beat themselves raw trying to swim up the spillway. The dam also prevented endangered green sturgeon from navigating their way upriver to spawn.

On their downriver migration, juvenile salmon were routinely sucked into the dam's outlet and flushed into irrigation canals, end-

ing up as fertilizer mash in orchards and rice fields. To counter this, a battery of huge, rotating drumlike screens were placed at the head of a canal, which diverted fingerlings from the canal into a tunnel that went several hundred yards underground to a concrete pillbox. There the fish were released to resume their migration to the sea. In the maelstrom below the dam, however, these small fish were easy prey for voracious pikeminnows, a native species growing up to two feet long, and predatory striped bass and American shad.

Some fishery experts have called the Red Bluff Diversion Dam the single most important cause of salmon declines on the Sacramento River. In 2010, a project was finally approved and funded to resolve the problems of fish passage. As of 2012, newly installed pumps were sending water into the irrigation canals, precluding the need to lower the dam's gates and thus allowing salmon, steelhead, and green sturgeon unencumbered passage upriver. The dam is now obsolete.

Beyond Shasta and Red Bluff Diversion dams, other dams were built on tributaries

vision of the National Oceanic and Atmospheric Administration) concluded from its studies that "striped bass are without a doubt one of the main predators of salmon smolts in the Sacramento River." The DFG estimates stripers could be eating as much as twenty-five percent to fifty percent of endangered winter-run and threatened spring-run salmon each year.

A dead green sturgeon with mangled tail, the result of trying to get past the Red Bluff Diversion Dam. Doug Killam.

throughout the system, including the American River, Feather River, Clear Creek, Battle Creek, Butte Creek, and Deer Creek, among others. Each of these was a historical migration avenue for salmon and steelhead. All told, over ninety-five percent of salmon-rearing habitat in the Sacramento system was eliminated.

The Delta's decline has further impacted the well-being of salmon and other native species. As presented in the last chapter, ineffective water management remains a central cause. Scientists also point to poor ocean conditions, which reduce salmon food sources. Added reasons are angler catches and predation by other fish—in particular, striped bass.

The National Marine Fisheries Service (a di-

Such conclusions are vehemently countered by sport fishing groups, including the California Sportfishing Protection Alliance, which argue that striped bass have coexisted with salmon on the river since they were introduced over a hundred years ago with few adverse effects.

Fishery biologist and expert Dr. Peter Moyle concludes from his research that "the contribution of striped bass to fish declines is not certain. Overall, the key to restoring populations of desirable species…is to return the Delta to being a more variable, estuarine environment."

To redress other problems, varied measures have been pursued. With dams impeding gravel dispersion from the upper watershed, the DFG dumps loads of gravel each year on the river's banks in selected places below Keswick Dam so high flows can take the precious rocks downriver, substituting quarries and dump trucks for nature's work.

To counter warm waters created by Shasta Lake, especially pronounced during drought years, a temperature control device was constructed at Shasta Dam in 1997. This multi-million-dollar device consists of a steel enclosure with sliding gates called shutters, which surround the power plant's intakes, thus enabling an operator to withdraw deeper, colder water at bottom depths for release into the river. This allows the river's water to be maintained at colder temperatures more conducive to salmon, particularly the prized winter-run strain.

Salmon Runs Imperiled

Despite all the technological efforts to stem the collapse of salmon, and various strategies implemented or proposed to counter possible causes, salmon runs in the Sacramento system are imperiled. This is especially true for the more valued wild fish.

The winter-run is designated "endangered." From nearly 100,000 returning fish in the late 1960s, fewer than 200 came back in the early 1990s. The numbers rebounded to a yearly average of 13,700 fish from 2004 to 2006. However, they have since dropped below 3,000. Denied from reaching their historical waters, the salmon's primeval genes are surely being diluted. Interbreeding with salmon from other runs is also probable due to mixing in confined waters. According to Moyle, what is being artificially maintained is largely a "museum run" of fish that in all probability will not survive.

The spring-run also depended on the colder waters of upper waterways and was effectively curtailed by Shasta Dam. Once a robust run, it collapsed to only a handful of fish almost exclusively confined to Butte, Deer, and Mill creeks in Butte and Tehama counties. As will be discussed later in this chapter, it has rebounded, but with wide yearly fluctuations. The spring-run is designated "threatened," but it is more accurately endangered.

The late fall-run seems the most resilient and stable, with numbers ranging from 10,000 to 18,000 in recent years. Due to their longer residency in both ocean and fresh water, these stream-type Chinook grow to be the largest and most fecund salmon in the Sacramento River. They spawn and rear primarily in the river above the Coleman National Fish Hatchery, which makes tracking their numbers more difficult.

The fall-run is now the dominant one in the system, and these are mainly hatchery-reared fish. The unnatural seasonal flows and remaining habitat are most conducive to these ocean-type Chinook, which spawn mainly in lowland reaches of big rivers and their tributaries. For decades it was the backbone of the West Coast fishing industry in both oceans and rivers, providing ninety percent of Chinook salmon caught in California.

The numbers of returning salmon to Coleman have plummeted, from 750,000 in 2002 to an astounding low of 8,300 in 2009. Returns bounced back up to 42,000 in 2011 and over 100,000 in 2012, suggesting that perhaps the collapse has bottomed out. Such measly numbers compared to those of the past demonstrate that hatchery-reared fish also require healthy river and ocean conditions to survive.

Due to the salmon crash, ocean commercial and sport fishing was closed in 2008 and 2009 (angling restrictions were also tightened on the Sacramento). This move precipitated the loss of an estimated 23,000 fishing-related jobs and the grounding of nearly 1,200 commercial fishing boats. The total loss was estimated at $2.8 billion.

Coleman fish managers have taken drastic

steps to prevent such future losses. Beginning in 2007, they started trucking approximately 300,000 three-inch juvenile salmon 200 miles to San Pablo Bay. This avoids the perils of having young salmon journey down the river and pass through the Delta, a sad state to be reached. Officials expected only one and one-half percent to come back to the Sacramento, and only three-quarters of a percent—3,900 fish—to return to Coleman. But since this trucking program was mainly to improve ocean numbers and reinvigorate sport fishing, it was curtailed in 2012 due to the improving picture.

It's now evident that the widely touted "cheap power" which dams produced in their halcyon days really exacted an enormously high price—the collapse of salmon runs throughout the Northwest. "New power" generated by dams replaced the "old power" generated by salmon. Spread of agriculture and creation of industries—of unquestionable value, to be sure—further stole from the fisheries. These did not have to be either/or choices. Such development should have been carried out alongside healthy rivers and salmon runs, the values of which are also unquestionable.

"The Creator put salmon in the rivers for a reason," said Caleen Sisk, principal chief and spiritual leader of the Winnemem Wintu. It's urgent to preserve what salmon still remain in the system—and in a much more crucial and ambitious undertaking, try to restore a semblance of what used to be.

Bringing Salmon Back

Timothy Egan succinctly defined the issue: "Rivers without salmon have lost the life source of the area...a river without salmon is a body without a soul."

It's also true that salmon without healthy rivers are lost. But provide free-flowing, clean water, and miracles can happen. Open up a river channel, return more water, restore riparian growth, eliminate pollutants, and a formerly sick river will replenish, cleanse, and ultimately heal itself. The presence of salmon in a river will tell humans how well they are doing.

John McCullah, champion of watershed restoration, including Sulphur Creek, shown here—a small tributary to the Sacramento where salmon used to spawn. Bob Madgic.

A movement to demolish dams—an about-face shift on these monolithic structures—is lending a major boost to river and salmon restoration. Bruce Babbitt, then-Secretary of the Interior under President Bill Clinton, spearheaded this shift. He traveled to and evaluated dams across the country, asking, "Is this dam still serving its purpose? Do the benefits justify the destruction of fish runs and drying up of rivers?" In several cases the clear answer was no, and dams started coming down.

One—McCormack-Saeltzer Dam—was on Clear Creek in Shasta County, at one time supporting three of the four Sacramento salmon runs. Like so many other waterways, it was ravaged by gold mining. (Huge piles of sterile dredger tailings still defile large areas.) The dam

Zeke Grader, Executive Director of PCFFA and longtime protector of California's native fish. Courtesy of Pacific Coast Federation of Fishermen's Associations.

stopped salmon from any farther migration and effectively ended runs in the waterway. In 2000, it was taken down, with Babbitt delivering the first sledgehammer blow. The channel has since been dredged of accumulated silt, riparian foliage planted, flows increased, and gravel added. Clear Creek is now seeing the returns of significant salmon and steelhead runs.

Restoration efforts on Battle Creek have been even more ambitious. Originating on the western slopes of Lassen Peak, Battle Creek

flows some forty-two miles through a deep canyon before emptying into the Sacramento River. Its clear, cold water comes largely from aquifers generously fed by snowmelt and stored in porous, water-filtering volcanic rock. In 1901, while salmon and steelhead were thriving in Battle Creek, developers sought to cash in on its hydroelectric potential. A moderately large dam—Wildcat Dam—and a cluster of smaller dams were built in the early 1900s on the north and south forks of Battle Creek to generate electricity.

After years of meetings, the Greater Battle Creek Watershed Working Group, consisting of the Battle Creek Watershed Conservancy and multiple governmental agencies, reached agreement to remove Wildcat Dam and four others in a massive project costing $80 million. One of the largest anadromous fish restoration efforts in North America, it will restore approximately forty-two miles of habitat in Battle Creek plus another six miles in tributaries. According to estimates, the project should yield about 2,500 spring-run Chinook and 2,000 winter-run Chinook. Sharon Paquin-Gilmore, chair of the Watershed Group, says, "What our community has learned is that a healthy watershed is vital to all of us living and working here, and salmon are vital to making the watershed healthy."

Farther south, Butte, Mill, and Deer creeks each host spring-run Chinook. The runs in Mill and Deer are minimal; the run up Butte is the most significant. From the volcanic cliffs surrounding this fast-flowing creek, one can peer down at salmon holding in deep summer pools. In fall, they will spawn at the tails of the pools or move downstream to larger expanses of gravel. Allen Harthorn, executive director of Friends of Butte Creek, aptly calls it "the last best run of wild salmon in California."

In 1987, only fourteen fish returned to Butte Creek, prompting a desperate effort to stave

Flows at Clear Creek now run strongly after removal of the McCormack–Saeltzer Dam. Courtesy of Western Shasta Resource Conservation District.

DFG biologist moving a captured Chinook salmon to better habitat on Butte Creek. Harry Morse.

Oren Nardi, Redding teenager who works to preserve salmon and other native fish. Bob Madgic.

off extinction. Approximately $40 million was spent by private interests and the state and federal governments on a variety of projects. Flows increased in 1992, and by 1995 the run had jumped back up to 7,500. The major stroke was the removal of five small dams. Fish ladders were built and numerous screens inserted to keep salmon out of water-diversion pipes. A coalition of groups also purchased water rights from local ranchers to put more water back in the river during key salmon migration months.

In 1998, 20,000 spring-run salmon returned, indicating good progress. But that number dropped to 11,000 in 2008, and then fell dramatically to just under 2,000 in 2010. The run rebounded with 10,000 in 2012. Two remaining dams in the upper creek continue to adversely affect fish returns, however. The future of spring-run salmon in the Sacramento system largely depends on what happens in Butte Creek.

As more waterways are freed up and cleansed, the restorative power of flowing water will lead to their rebirth and that of their anadromous stalwarts. The undertaking is crucial, the probabilities unknown. What is known is that salmon require variations and options in migration times and pathways, waters, spawning

Salmon People

Few rivers in the Sacramento watershed offer salmon cold, clean water like that of the McCloud. And none want them back there more than the Winnemem Wintu, who call themselves "salmon people." They see this as a spiritual quest, believing it is their duty to

Caleen Fisk, spiritual leader of the Winnemem Wintu and defender of salmon. Marc Dadigan.

sites, and stays in fresh and salt water. Research has shown that juveniles grow bigger faster if they are able to spend time in seasonally inundated floodplains, even flooded agricultural fields, that create new channels alongside the main river. Such variability produces resilient fish, capable of overcoming the many obstacles humankind has placed before them.

The matter could not be more important. For as a Winnemem Wintu prophesy holds: *When there are no salmon, there will be no people.*

return their "relatives" to the river where they once lived together in harmony. To accomplish this, they are pursuing a plan to establish a hatchery on the upper McCloud, rearing the same genetic species of fish that once came to this river—the winter-run salmon, which is on the verge of extinction. In the 1870s, eggs from these fish were sent to New Zealand, where they became established as "Rakaia salmon." (In New Zealand, the salmon spawn all seasons, so no distinct "runs" are distinguished there.) The

Winnemem swimming below McCloud River's Middle Falls to replicate what their revered salmon once did. Marc Dadigan.

Winnemem want to bring these descendants of their sacred fish back from New Zealand and raise them in the hatchery.

If the plan succeeds, the newly reared salmon will be imprinted with the McCloud's waters and guided to enter the Sacramento. To have them return to the McCloud, the Winnemem propose connecting the Sacramento and the McCloud by Dry Creek that flows alongside Shasta Lake and empties into Cow Creek, a tributary to the Sacramento. A quarter-mile man-made channel connecting Dry Creek with Shasta Lake would be built. McCloud water would be flushed down it so returning salmon can follow their spawning senses to find their way back. From the connecting channel, the salmon would enter the southwest corner of Shasta Lake. Then, in the words of tribal leader Sisk: "Once they will get a whiff of their spawning waters, the salmon will find their way home."

So true for all salmon.

Snow geese. Peter Park.

CHAPTER EIGHT

Advance of Conservation

"Over increasingly large areas of the United States, spring now comes unheralded by the return of the birds, and the early mornings are strangely silent where once they were filled with the beauty of bird song."

—*Rachel Carson*

WITH ITS BROAD FLOOD PLAIN, LUSH riparian forests, thousands of acres of wetlands, profuse populations of birds, amphibians, mammals, fishes, and other biota, and a marvelously complex river carrying nutrients from the mountains to the sea, the Sacramento Valley was once one of the most prolific bio-regions in the world.

This extraordinary network of life has been in steep decline—the reasons clear yet complex. It is a story that is reflected in part by what has transpired with one of the valley's most prominent creatures—birds.

Creation of Refuges

For thousands of years, millions of waterfowl populated the Sacramento Valley. Winter flooding produced vast wetlands that, along with numerous grasslands and forests, supported a profusion of birds and other wildlife. Toward the end of the nineteenth century, farmland had replaced much of this natural topography. Hundreds of thousands of waterfowl—Canada geese the most numerous—flocked to these enticing wheat fields and ravaged them. Farmers

and hired hands tried to "herd" the birds away, often resorting to shooting sprees, but they fought a losing battle.

Late in the nineteenth century, rice was introduced to the region. The flooded rice fields quickly attracted multitudinous birds, particularly ducks like pintails and mallards, which devoured huge swaths of the crop. Some species altered their migration timetables to feed on the rice. And being night feeders, the ducks were not easily dispersed. Snow geese, which had previously wintered and fed primarily in estuaries, also quickly adapted to a diet of rice. Landowners grew increasingly desperate to ward off the birds and get money for their crops.

Relief came from FDR's New Deal. In January 1937, the federal government purchased the 10,775-acre Spalding Ranch located between the towns of Willows and Maxwell—labeled by some the "most famous goose sanctuary" on the West Coast. The U.S. Fish and Wildlife Service, aided by the Civilian Conservation Corps, flooded the alkaline lands, parched lakes and vernal pools, pastures, and former rice fields,

Greater white-fronted geese. Mike Peters.

turning them into wetlands. It was designated the Sacramento National Wildlife Refuge. The birds now had a place designed especially for them to hang out and eat.

In the next decades the government created three more wildlife refuges: Colusa (1945), Sutter (1945), and Delevan (1962). Each provided wetlands and grasslands for waterfowl; each sought to reduce the toll on crops. A fifth refuge, the Sacramento River Refuge, was added in 1989. In all, the five refuges comprise the Sacramento National Wildlife Refuge Complex, which also includes three wildlife management areas: North Central Valley, Willow Creek–Lurline, and Butte Sink.

The refuges must be actively managed to remain wetlands. Water is brought in; the ground is disked; grass and plants are mowed; burns are prescribed. In spring, the refuges slowly drain from seasonal flooding and plants re-sprout on the moist, exposed soil. The lands dry out over the summer. In the fall they are re-flooded, just in time for the first wave of migrating birds. The results are wetlands, vernal pools, alkali meadows, grasslands, riparian vegetation, and refurbished wildlife populations, all contributing to the health of the valley and river flowing through it.

As many as 250 species of birds and fifty species of mammals, reptiles, and amphibians

The Gray Lodge Wildlife Refuge shown here is a state refuge managed by the DFG. It is located about sixty miles north of Sacramento. Mike Peters.

occupy these sanctuaries across the seasons. Most numerous are the wintering concentrations of 500,000 to 750,000 ducks and 200,000 geese. Birds still consume nearby farm crops, but most of the rice is harvested before the droves of wintering waterfowl arrive. The rice ponds augment the birds' nesting and foraging habitat, and in some cases act as hunting outposts.

Although the refuges and birds are integrally connected to the Sacramento River, the whole network is only as strong as any one element. Above all, the integrity of the river had to be renewed and sustained for everything to flourish as it should.

Case for Conservation.

Beyond wildlife refuges, no significant conservation initiatives addressed declines in the Sacramento River going into the second half of the twentieth century. Indeed, the opposite was true. Pressures intensified to further constrict and "armor" the river with levees and rip rap, and send its water elsewhere. Farms and urban development straitjacketed the river almost to its banks in long stretches. Southern California water demands were insatiable, with more housing tracts, shopping centers, and golf courses. Agricultural water needs—already using eighty percent of federal allotments—were unceasing. More dams kept getting built.

Development trumped concern over the Sacramento River's declining health. To reverse course, individuals and organizations began trumpeting the need for more environmental protections. The consequences of a century and a half of rampant resource exploitation and industrial production were all too appar-

bereft of birds. Then-Secretary of the Interior Stewart Udall contended these very successes brought about a "quiet crisis of conservation," whereby waste products befouled the land and introduced "frightening new forms of erosion." Aldo Leopold in his book *A Sand County Almanac* argued on behalf of a "land ethic," where

A wood duck. Their numbers in the Sacramento Valley are a fraction of what they used to be. Mike Peters.

ent: widespread destruction of natural habitat, disappearing species, and polluted air, land, and water.

Much of this contamination accompanied scientific and technological advances, which had ushered in an "age of abundance." New chemicals increased agricultural yields; new technologies produced more efficient automobiles and airplanes; scientific breakthroughs created new energy sources. Biologist Rachel Carson, however, saw such developments creating an "age of poisons" and a "silent spring"

lands and organisms are treated as a "community," and humans act to preserve its integrity, stability, and beauty.

Such revelations and reasoning resonated with Americans, inducing Congress to pass a wave of environmental legislation: The Clean Air Act (1963); The Wilderness Act (1964); The Land and Water Conservation Fund (1964); The Wild and Scenic Rivers Act (1968); The National Trails System Acts (1968); The Clean Water Act (1972); and The Endangered Species Act (1973). Legal and ecological foundations for protecting the nation's most vital resources—air, forests, water, native species—had been established. Further, a federal agency—the Environmental Protection Agency (EPA)—was created in 1970, charged with protecting human health and the environment by writing and enforcing governmental regulations.

The passage of these laws with bipartisan support was monumental. But they did not ensure protection, for conservation battles are usually fought issue by issue. One crushing defeat was a treasured nine-mile section of the Stanislaus River, a prime whitewater stretch flowing in a rich limestone canyon in the central Sierra Nevada. The nation's dam-building era was fading, yet one more remained on the books—the New Melones Dam. If built, it would create a twenty-four-mile-long reservoir that would inundate the famed upper canyon. River stalwarts like Jerry Meral, David Kay, and Mark Dubois launched an organization, Friends of the River (FOR), to "save the Stan." Despite an outpouring of opposition, the New Melones was completed in 1979. Although FOR lost that fight, it would grow into a powerful force in California's and the nation's water wars. (Two more proposed large dams in California, one on the Tuolumne and one on the North Fork American—the infamous "Auburn Dam"—were beaten back.)

Another emerging river champion was Tim Palmer. Recounting the loss of the Stanislaus, he wrote: "A wild river shows life like no other place. Simple truths of the earth are seen

Pintail ducks, a prime prey for hunters. Mike Peters.

more easily here. That helps to make this place [Stanislaus Canyon] powerful." Utilizing his eloquent pen and striking photographs, Palmer would go on to make the case for wild rivers across the nation.

The Sacramento River was left out of the environmental surge, at least initially. What actually resurfaced was a longstanding idea for intercepting the river's water and sending it via a forty-three-mile "peripheral canal" directly to the aqueduct at Tracy, thereby bypassing the Delta entirely. Such a canal had been a top priority of water interests for decades, primarily to deliver more water to the ever-growing Los Angeles region.

When Governor Pat Brown instigated the California Water Project to fuel growth in Southern California, his grand design featured this controversial water diversion. But funds ran out before the peripheral canal could be built, and it was temporarily shelved.

A severe and prolonged drought at the end of the 1970s spurred the California Senate to resurrect it and pass a bill authorizing the canal. Backing it was the son of Pat Brown, Jerry Brown, who won the governorship in 1975 holding views that "less is more" and "small is beautiful." Not in this case, however. He found himself caught between his strong environmental leanings and desire to please the powerful water lobbies, as well as complete his father's plan. At the outset, water interests predictably supported the bill; a few highly placed Brown supporters did as well. Many citizens saw the canal as a Southern California water grab. Opponents gathered sufficient signatures to place a referendum to stop the canal on a statewide ballot in 1980.

Ironically, both environmentalists and a few powerful agricultural growers supported the referendum. The environmentalists opposed the removal of more water from the Delta; the

Tim Palmer, one of the country's staunchest defenders of rivers. Ann Vileisis.

growers opposed Brown's accompanying proposal—designed to mollify the environmentalists—to designate several Northern California rivers as "wild and scenic," which would protect them from dams. Both groups fought the bill, and it met with a resounding defeat.

Despite this reprieve, the Sacramento River possessed few protections from similar or other degrading moves. The main safeguard for rivers is the federal Wild and Scenic Rivers Act. (California passed its own Wild and Scenic Act in 1972.) Neither has been applied to any part of the Sacramento, including the Upper Sac, a natural candidate. The two laws that do offer protections are the Clean Water Act and Endangered Species Act.

For decades, runoffs containing pollutants, pesticides, trace metals, mercury, dioxins, among other contaminants from countless sources, entered most waterways, ending up as well in estuaries and bays. Such pollutants—particularly mercury—devastated marine organisms like shellfish and the animals that eat them, such as otters. They posed health risks to humans, especially those who consume lots of fish. Unnaturally high water temperatures can

dates that to recover an endangered species, all of its "critical habitat"—land, water, and air—must be identified and protected. The ESA thus protects and restores natural habitat, like old-growth forests, riparian lands, and free-flowing waterways, usually with vehement opposition

A protective tundra swan looks out for her cygnets. Mike Peters.

also cause bacteria to flourish and unhealthy algae to grow. The Clean Water Act requires water quality standards and sets the stage for lawsuits when they are not met. (The Stockton-based California Sportfishing Protection Alliance under leader Bill Jennings has been especially active in this regard.) Thanks to this act, many sources of pollutants up and down the river have been eliminated, with much cleaner water as a result.

The Endangered Species Act (ESA) offers more encompassing protections. The law man-

from extraction industry people and property rights advocates.

California passed it own endangered species act in 1984, adding the category "Species of Special Concern"—ones that could decline to threatened or endangered status. With the exception of Hawaii, California has more endangered species and double the number proposed than any other state. More species in the Sacramento Valley have been listed under state law than under federal law, attesting to the state's commitment to its environment.

Return of Snow Geese

A VISITOR to the central Sacramento River on a winter day is apt to be serenaded by dissonant honks, cackles, and peeps from geese, ducks, cranes, swans, and more. Countless downy white snow geese usually dominate the scene. Throngs of these graceful birds sometimes burst to the skies with a thunderous rush of wings and gabbling cacophony. Then high above, in striking formations or randomized masses, thousands of them will appear like white specks of paint flung from a wide brush against a blue canvas. The sheer energy of this moving tapestry is not only seen and heard, but felt.

The migratory snow goose is a visitor from far northern Canada and the Arctic, from places such as Banks Island, Queen Maud Gulf, and Wrangle Island. The latter, a rugged, pristine place, is about ninety miles northeast of Siberia and several hundred miles northwest of Alaska. Combining jagged cliffs with open expanses mantled in snow 240 days or more each year, the island teems with animals and over fifty bird species. Its fledgling snow geese must survive brutally cold weather, disease, and predation by other birds and mammals. Arctic foxes often consume well over half of the eggs laid.

As the temperature drops in early autumn, snow geese head south. Frequently at an altitude of 3,000 feet, they fly nonstop for seventy hours at speeds averaging forty to fifty miles per hour. Their path is known as the Pacific Flyway. Reaching northeastern California, the geese often stop first at Tule Lake—an oasis of shallow, reed-filled waters. Then they depart for the Sacramento Valley wetlands, today only a small fraction of their historic acreage. Irrigation ditches and flooded rice fields augment foraging opportunities. Many birds of several species end their journey there, while others press on to warmer locations in Mexico and beyond.

Snow geese. Mike Peters.

With the ESA in place, birds and fish and trees and plants finally possessed power, not only to fend off extinction, but to defend their surroundings.

Sacramento's Birds

Birds are highly sensitive to the health of places where they live or visit. Among species native to the Sacramento Valley are the yellow-billed returns to California in summer to nest in thick stands of young willows and other understory foliage on point bars and river banks. Their foods of choice—tree frogs and large insects— appear for only a short time, prompting these highly secretive birds (more often heard than seen) to breed quickly and their young to develop rapidly. In late summer, the cuckoos leave California and head back to South America.

Yellow-billed cuckoo, a shy neo-tropical visitor. Claire de Beauvoir.

magpie, which prefers groves of tall trees along rivers and near open areas; the tri-colored blackbird, which like its cousin, the red-winged blackbird, utilizes marshes; the Nuttall's woodpecker, which lives in riparian plant communities and deciduous oak woodlands; and the least bell's vireo, a shy, secretive, silver-tongued bird that occupies riparian woodlands.

Many neo-tropical migratory birds visit the Sacramento. The western yellow-billed cuckoo

Another migratory bird is the Swainson's hawk, one of the most strikingly marked raptors. In vast open grasslands they hunt voles and other small mammals, and insects and birds they take on the wing. They require large trees—cottonwoods, oaks, sycamores, and willows—for nesting sites. These habitats are ever shrinking.

One of the most captivating bird species is the swallow. The Sacramento River corridor is

Swainson's hawk, one of the most beautiful of raptors and a threatened species. Christopher Christie.

home to several species of swallows, including barn swallow, tree swallow, cliff swallow, and bank swallow. Voracious consumers of insects, these beguiling birds winter in South America and return to the Sacramento each spring, often to the same nests. Some pairs mate for life.

Of these, the bank swallow possesses a special but tenuous connection to the Sacramento River.

In early spring, these smallest of all swallow species arrive in the river corridor to build nests and mate. Sparrow-like in size, the adult has a grayish-brown mantle, rump and wing coverts. Its notched tail is entirely brown or brown with pale endings. The throat is white and contrasts sharply with the distinct brown breast band and grayish-brown crown.

Bank swallows are highly social, joining with hundreds—sometimes thousands—of their brethren to form colonies. To nest, they

seek sandy or dirt soil on vertical banks, formed primarily when a river carves out new channels as it turns and twists. Arriving first, a male will select a site and begin burrowing into the upper third of the bank to avoid predators. It secures itself against the bank with its claws, spreading out its tail for added support, and then uses its tiny, conical bill to pick and scratch the soil until there is enough space to fit inside. It continues to dig with its bill and claws, ferreting out a burrow parallel to the ground, sometimes as long as five feet. If a pair of swallows already exists, the female will keep watch at the site entrance while her partner digs. Lacking a mate, the male will attempt to attract a female by singing and ruffling his head and throat feathers in a showy display. After the burrow is completed, the female builds the nest deep inside, using grass, rootlets, weeds, and feathers to line it. She incubates typically four to five eggs, often

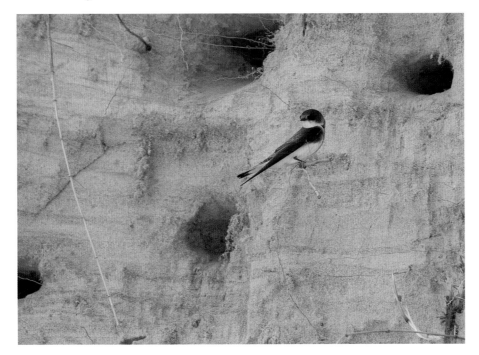

Bank swallow.
Jim Barber.

with the male's help. Eighteen to twenty-four days after hatching, the bank swallow fledglings leave the nest.

Watching a pair of swallows mating, nabbing insects, or soaring about is to witness a dazzling ballet. To see hundreds of these highly energized, seemingly exuberant birds is like watching a sky full of meteors. Feeding and foraging almost dawn to dusk, they dart and swoop and zoom over water and nearby fields, snatching mosquitoes, ants, bees, wasps, flies, and beetles. A typical swallow will catch about eight thousand insects a day, constituting about four hundred meals. To feed their young, swallows roll their catch into a compact ball and carry it in their throats back to the nest.

Birds have long signaled the dire state of the Sacramento Valley. In 1986, researchers intensively studied bank swallows along the

Sacramento River and estimated that it supported approximately seventy percent of California's breeding population. (Due to habitat eradication in Southern California, bank swallows there have been long gone.) Results from annual surveys show a fluctuating population

Bank swallows depend on dirt banks for nesting. Dawn Garcia.

that has not recovered to its 1986 numbers. Instead they have showed dramatic declines. With the meandering of the Sacramento in check from armoring across long stretches, the bank swallow's habitat of fresh-cut banks is ever shrinking. Today it is a threatened species.

The yellow-billed cuckoo is an endangered species, clinging to existence in isolated forested sites along the river. Populations have gone from 70,000 breeding pairs in California in the early twentieth century, to only 30 to 50 breeding pairs by the start of the 2000s. The least bell's vireo, once one of California's most numerous birds, has been reduced to less than 300 pairs. The Swainson's hawk is a threatened species under California's law, with perhaps 500 pairs remaining.

The main culprit behind waning bird numbers is loss of multi-faceted habitat: riparian forests, old-growth trees, woodlands, diverse canopy and understory, marshes, and diverse land forms. Where such a complex mosaic still exists, it is apt to be limited and fragmented. Birds (and other animals) need broad swaths of habitat, sometimes totaling thousands of acres, to breed and forage. When such habitat breadth is lacking and conditions become crowded, they are more vulnerable to disease, predation, and loss of genetic diversity. Their populations plummet.

Beyond Birds

Although birds are among the clearest beacons for spotlighting environmental decay, the entire spectrum of plant and animal life is at risk when conditions decline.

The valley elderberry longhorn beetle depends on elderberry bushes for its survival. River Partners.

Numbers of the giant garter snake like this one are in steep decline. U.S. Fish & Wildlife Service.

Every habitat along the Sacramento River holds at-risk species. The threatened valley elderberry longhorn beetle lives in riparian woodlands. Before mating, these colorful beetles—the female has dark metallic green forewings with red margins, while the male's are primarily red with dark green spots—eat elderberry bush foliage. The female then lays her eggs in crevices of the bark. Upon hatching, the larvae tunnel into a woody interior where they will spend one to two years eating the pulp—their sole food source. Not surprisingly, sightings of this one-inch-long beetle are rare; adult exit holes provide the only evidence of their presence. Decline of elderberry bushes due to riparian losses has made them a threatened species (this designation is under review at the time of this publication) and the beetles' critical habitat

of elderberry bushes is protected. Where they exist, development has been checked.

Another is the giant garter snake. Up to five feet long, with black spots checkering its brown, yellow-lined body, this shy creature lives in marshes, seasonal wetlands, and sloughs, feeding on small fish, tadpoles, and frogs. It often basks in the sun on willow branches over the water's edge, partially screened by weeds and tules. As its habitat keeps shrinking, it is more susceptible to predators, like skunks, raccoons, foxes, and domestic cats. Pesticides also exact a harsh toll. The observer who catches a glimpse of this arresting, elusive reptile is fortunate.

Shrinking forests and woodlands have left many mammal species with little territory to roam and forage. Mountain lions, bobcats, Sacramento Valley red foxes, and brush rabbits

Bats

O NE POPULAR winged creature occupying the Yolo Wildlife Area is a flying mammal. Observers flock to the region to witness the evening fly-out of Mexican free-tailed bats from their daytime haunts under the Yolo Causeway bridge, just west of Sacramento. This migratory bat species colonizes in the long "cave" beneath the roadway and numbers more than 250,000. (Other bat species in the region—there are seventeen bat species in all of Northern California—include the red bat, Townsend's big-eared bat, and Yuma myotis bat.)

Approximately 1250 bat species exist, constituting twenty percent of all mammal species. The only flying mammal, they can be as small as a bumblebee and as large as a house cat. Bats are the most abundant of all species in rainforests. They pollinate flowers and plants

A Mexican free-tailed bat. This species is the speedster of the bat world.
Copyright © Merlin D. Tuttle, Bat Conservation International.

like bananas, mangoes, cashews, and dates; they also spread their seeds. Highly sensitive to changes in landscapes, they are excellent indicators of biodiversity and habitat health. Due to losses and degradation in places where they live—such as caves—and the forests where their food is located, more than twenty-five percent of bat species worldwide are threatened with extinction.

Contrary to myth, bats are good for human and environmental health, mainly by controlling insects. Interestingly, they catch insects by trapping them with their tail membranes as they swoop and dive. A bat can consume up to three times its body weight in one night—five hundred to one thousand insects per hour. They are the top predators of flying nocturnal insects that can ravage crops, such as moths, beetles, and leaf hoppers. Bats save farmers billions of dollars each year in crop savings and lower pesticide costs.

Mexican free-tailed bats are medium-sized bats, about three and one-half inches long and weighing slightly less than half an ounce. They vary from dark brown to gray. Their tails extend beyond their body and make up almost half their length, accounting for the species' name. Their wings are long, narrow, and pointed, equipping them for rapid flight—the "speedsters" of the bat world. They have been clocked flying (with tail winds) at sixty miles per hour, and at altitudes over ten thousand feet, an environment in which few other organisms, including humans, can survive.

During summer evenings, swarms of these distinctive bats leave their roosts under the Yolo Causeway at dusk in search of food, streaking the sky in dense ribbons. Thousands of flapping wings create a visual feast and musical din. Though bats have better night vision than humans, they locate their food using echolocation (also called biosonar), meaning they emit constant, brief frequency calls and listen to the echoes to locate even the tiniest of insects. At dawn, the free-tails return in displays as spectacular as those in the evening.

The United Nations declared 2011 the Year of the Bat.

Mexican free-tailed bats leave their nests under the Yolo Causeway at dusk in dense throngs throughout the summer. Dave Feliz.

A DFG officer releases a banded pintail duck so their numbers and locations can be tracked. Dave Feliz.

have fewer wild places to be the wild animals they are. Their continued presence in the Sacramento Valley is at stake.

Some of the most prominent and significant threatened species swim in the Sacramento River itself. These include the green sturgeon, Sacramento splittail, Central Valley steelhead, Chinook salmon, and delta smelt. The health of the river can be gauged by the state of its native fish, and the picture is dismal here as well.

Threatened species represent a last fortress for protecting the Sacramento River from more water diversions, losses of riparian foliage, rip rapping, and other inflictions. Any project, whether public or private, must adhere to stipulations of the state or federal endangered species acts. Once an organism gets designated, these stipulations become overriding, so groups try to avoid a listing. Property rights advocates, including landowners with the best interests of the river at heart, are often leery about having a species listed, fearing possible restrictions on their lands. Environmental organizations, knowing the power of the ESA for staving off another extinction or habitat setback, often seek listings as the last resort.

Critics have contended that such protections of species, whether fish or beetles or bushes, should not take precedence over the well-being of humans, like farmers, loggers, landowners, and developers. Such concerns ignore the vital connections between human welfare and that of plants and animals. Albert Einstein bluntly stated the case: "If the bee disappeared off the surface of the globe then man would only have four years of life left. No more bees, no more pollination, no more plants, no more animals, no more man." This speaks to the import of each and every life form, as exemplified by countless medical and scientific breakthroughs, food and commercial products, recreational opportunities, and economic returns, many often traceable to obscure plant and animal species.

The presence and preservation of the many species that call the Sacramento Valley home reflects in large part on its health, and that of the river. Each and every organism contributes.

Of North American birds, the America white pelican has the second longest wingspan (behind the California condor). The pelican occupies bodies of water and wetlands throughout the Sacramento Valley. Unlike its cousin, the gray pelican, the white pelican doesn't dive for its food. It uses its long beak to pluck small fish and other foods from down in the water. Bob Madgic.

Today, farmlands have replaced most of the riparian forests along the Sacramento River. Bruce King.

CHAPTER NINE

Preserve, Restore, Educate

"The care of the Earth is our most ancient and most worthy, and after all, our most pleasing responsibility. To cherish what remains of it, and to foster its renewal, is our only hope."

—*Wendell Berry*

BY 1980, ONLY TWO PERCENT OF THE original riverside forest remained along the Sacramento. Long stretches were channelized and armored. Numbers of endangered and threatened species had surpassed fifty. Grizzly bears and gray wolves were long gone. Mountain lions were rare. Amphibian species, like the giant garter snake and blunt-nosed leopard lizard, were in steep decline. Numbers of forest and woodland bird species had plummeted. Populations of native fish species, particularly salmon, were in a long downward trend.

Restoring riparian habitat bolsters biodiversity. Payoffs extend far beyond wildlife. Ultimately, it's humans who can ill afford to have rivers stripped of riparian vegetation. Such foliage improves water and air quality by filtering out pollutants, including toxins from agricultural runoff, and by capturing carbon emissions. It reduces erosion and keeps silt from suffocating a waterway and smothering gravel beds needed for fish to spawn. It controls the ravages of flooding by anchoring trees and plants. It aerates soil in floodplains and allows water to accumulate and slowly percolate un-

derground to recharge aquifers, which in turn feed waterways and supply drinking water. It provides enriching recreational and educational opportunities.

The mission was clear and ambitious: riparian habitat where it still existed had to be preserved and where possible, restored. The clean water and endangered species acts were doing their part, but laws do not substitute for dedicated human efforts. And fortunately they were forthcoming.

Sacramento River Preservation Trust

By the start of the 1980s, a few individuals living in Chico were becoming increasingly frustrated with governmental efforts to harness the Sacramento instead of, as one said "adapting to its temperament." A love for rivers united them.

One was John Merz. Born in Texas, Merz made his way to California to complete his degree at Chico State University. He then worked for the Butte Environmental Council. Protecting the place where his family lived—especially the large river flowing nearby—became his priority.

The natural river meanders and forms long looping bends or "oxbows." Bruce King.

Today the river is straitjacketed by levees in many places, as shown here. Walt Simmons.

Another transplant was Steve Evans. Growing up in Southern California, he was captivated by the seasonal Mojave River flowing through the desert. As a child, he waded in its waters. Once in Chico, he grew passionate about canoeing and rafting the swift and churning rivers of Northern California.

The U.S. Army Corps of Engineers and California Reclamation Board had its own agenda for these waters. In 1983, under pressure from politically connected landowners, they sought, in the words of Merz, to "rip rap every bend between Red Bluff and Colusa," in effect making this long stretch into little more than a canal. Merz and Evans couldn't tolerate such a development.

At this same time, Tom Kraemer was pursuing a master's degree at Chico State University. His dissertation research showed that riparian vegetation could control flooding better than rip rap. He advanced the concept of a "meanderbelt," suggesting that government should buy enough land on either side of the river to push development and agriculture back a distance. This would allow the river to shift back and forth in meander fashion.

These findings caught the attention of Merz, who enlisted Evans and Kraemer to fight the rip rap project. They started an organization they called the Sacramento River Preservation Trust (SRPT). In its first major action, SRPT initiated the "Sacramento Bank Protection Project." Then, joined by other groups, SRPT sued the State Reclamation Board, the lead sponsor of the rip rapping project. In ruling on the lawsuit, the state court found that the environmental impact review prepared by the Reclamation Board insufficiently assessed the project's impacts on the environment and that the project could not go forward unless such studies were conducted. Because the results of such studies would surely be damning, the project was

John Merz, co-founder of the Sacramento River Preservation Trust and its director for almost thirty years. Tom Barrett.

Steve Evans, Conservation Director, Friends of the River. Barbara Murchison.

effectively killed. In the words of a triumphant Merz, the rip rap project was stopped "dead in the waters."

Since that time, Merz has led the work of SRPT. It has played a key role in advancing the natural values of the Sacramento River through conferences (including an annual "Snow Goose Festival"), workshops, field trips, and on occasion, lawsuits. It proceeds on the basis that the river is its own best teacher. The meanderbelt concept promoted by Kraemer took hold and is now standard strategy in restoration efforts. (Evans was later recruited by Friends of the River. As of this writing, he is its conservation director.)

Today's grey-bearded Merz remains impassioned about the detailed tapestry of life that characterizes the Sacramento. As he has stated: "The Sacramento is not just a river, it's a universe in and of itself."

The Nature Conservancy

Restoration projects sometimes entail a "Japanese gardening approach"—creation of a self-contained piece of restored river bend, riffle, vernal pool, or forest or grassland remnant. The result might be a nature sanctuary that is essentially an island. Wild critters and natural processes don't adhere to boundaries, however. That's why efforts are being made to restore and protect the Greater Yellowstone Ecosystem, ten times larger than Yellowstone National Park, which is itself larger than some states. Bringing back the Sacramento, too, requires massive, interconnected reaches of restored river and lands.

The Nature Conservancy (TNC) pursues such approaches. In 1988, TNC completed a "Sacramento River Preserve Design," which focused on eighteen outstanding riparian remnant sites—a "String of Pearls." It looked for willing sellers of riverside lands (private owners

own up to the shoreline while the state owns "under the river")—typically lands subject to flooding, active eroding, or with bad soil. Where land could not be purchased—TNC's primary conservation approach—it sometimes carried out a joint restoration project with a local farmer. While these projects proceeded, it became clear that piecemeal remnants were not the best answer.

The Nature Conservancy has since undertaken thirty-five restoration projects on thirteen properties between Red Bluff and Colusa. It wants to focus on the dynamics of the river's ecosystem in ten- to twenty-mile reaches. "We want to restore processes, not just place," said TNC's Mike Roberts. "For the first time, we're ignoring boundaries within our own parcels and thinking and planning on a landscape scale." The focus is on both land and river boundaries—where possible working on both sides of a river so meandering and floodplains can be reestablished.

The work of TNC developed into one of the largest riparian restoration projects in the United States. Called "The Sacramento River Project," its goal was to preserve or restore a continuous one-hundred-mile stretch between Red Bluff and Colusa, reviving ecosystem health and native species. Where riparian habitat exists, the project preserves it. Where absent—the dominant condition—the task is to bring back native vegetation while also eliminating and/or controlling non-native, invasive plant species, like yellow star thistle and Johnson grass. Since the roots of most native trees and plants have to reach the water table, land above ten feet typically won't restore naturally. In those cases, TNC utilizes standard farming techniques, like planting in rows and using drip irrigation to get the plants and trees established.

Plantings are carried out with specific species as targets. For example, sixteen "focal species"

Gregg Werner, Senior Project Director, Central Valley and Mountains, for The Nature Conservancy. Adrian Frediani.

of birds were identified as important indicators of riparian health. Each requires a specific habitat to thrive. The planner must know the needs of each target species and the growth characteristic of trees or shrubs in the design, and then attempt to establish that habitat.

The Point Reyes Bird Observatory, which has monitored thirty sites between Red Bluff and Sacramento, recommends a multi-species approach to riparian restoration rather than focusing only on endangered species. Working to help all sixteen focal species can ensure a more complex and healthier habitat, capable of supporting a wide array of wildlife.

By 2010, TNC had protected and restored the one-hundred-mile stretch of riverside habitat and was moving closer to creating its long-term goal of a thirty-thousand-acre wildlife corridor. While some private ownership and agricultural use will continue on these lands,

most of them will be publicly owned. To build local support, the conservancy remains committed to supporting agriculture and the local economy.

Project director for The Sacramento River Project is Gregg Werner, who manages a team of science, conservation, and support professionals in conjunction with numerous partners. Werner says: "A complex system like the Sacramento River displays the wonders of geomorphic processes and change at an accelerated pace that we can see and appreciate in a human rather than a geologic timeframe. I find this a totally absorbing experience."

River Partners

Who better to talk to farmers about land conservation than a fellow farmer? This was the origin of River Partners, a major restoration force for the Sacramento (and other Central Valley rivers). The initial impetus, however, was flood control.

One grower seeking relief from ongoing flooding of his prune and almond orchards in the small town of Gerber was Barney Flynn. He consulted his friend John Carlon, a nearby blueberry farmer and former employee of The Nature Conservancy. The two men devised a plan to plant native trees and shrubs between the river and an eroding levee to create a natural buffer. When rains came and the river breached its banks, the plan worked: vegetation anchored the soil and kept the river from storming into and over the levee.

With this flood-control strategy, Flynn and Carlon founded River Partners in 1998. They recruited ecologist Dr. Tom Griggs, another Nature Conservancy refugee. Waiting in the wings was a burgeoning clientele of farmers needing relief from flooding. River Partners convinced many of them that natural vegetation—elderberry, coyote bush, various willows, mule fat,

The seldom seen Sacramento Valley red fox is a native, unlike the introduced red fox that threatens the indigenous gray fox in other regions. Ben Sacks.

valley oak, box elder, sycamore—can prevent or minimize flooding, while producing many other benefits. Marginal land, for instance, becomes reinvigorated as natural habitat, attracting an array of birds and other wildlife.

River Partners found that flooding sometimes is desirable—that reconnecting the river with its floodplain by breaching nearby levees reduces pressure on other levees protecting populated or intensively farmed areas.

Griggs says: "Ecological flooding is a good thing. But the amount of flooding along many of our rivers is not natural, due in large part to human interference. Dams and reshaping of a river's natural course contribute to an unstable flood plain, putting not only the environment in danger, but the public as well. The lands we restore include farmland that is no longer economically viable—often due to flood prob-

lems. We work to contain floodwaters on many sites before they reach adjacent farmland or residential areas, where they can cause enormous damage. We take land 'left over' from agricultural operations and we put it back to use for wildlife, people and the environment."

The right balance has to be struck between the risks of flooding and risks from restricting flows and allowing water to build. Sometimes speeding up floodwaters may be the best strategy. For instance, most vegetation impedes flows and allows water to accumulate in places. This causes it to surge later at greater volume and breach levees. Recent studies found that a few native riparian shrubs with flexible canopies, like California blackberry, wild rose, sandbar willows, and mule fat, actually accelerate floodwaters. The swifter the water, the more these plants lay down, neither hindering nor clogging flood waters, while their roots still protect the soil and prevent erosion.

River Partners has innovated strategies for plant propagation and design. For a complex restoration plan, for instance, it uses "tiles," typically ten plants long and five rows wide. A plan might consist of thousands of tiles, with different plant species labeled, arranged, and clustered per tile. When planting a site, field crews follow the labels row by row, similar to paint-by-numbers art.

To attract wildlife, River Partners will often target an individual species in its planting strategies, particularly endangered ones. It planted wild roses and native blackberries together to form briar patches—excellent habitat for the endangered brush rabbit, for example. Another strategy combined willow clusters with a mugwort understory to attract the endangered least bell's vireo. Elderberry shrubs are included in plans whenever possible to provide habitat for the threatened elderberry beetle. This shrub also produces distinctive white flowers and fruit, which are food sources for wildlife.

Most River Partners undertakings today involve hundreds and thousands of acres, reconnecting habitats across large areas, much to the benefit of wildlife. Mountain lions, largely absent from the Sacramento Valley for decades, have repopulated areas. Flocks of wild turkeys forage through understory. Rare neo-tropical migrant songbirds, like the yellow-billed

River Partners' restoration projects often involve hundreds, even thousands, of acres. River Partners.

One way to clear land of unwanted vegetation like Himalayan blackberries is to bring in goats. River Partners.

cuckoo, are returning. Newly formed sloughs and oxbows in restored tracts burgeon with wood ducks, great blue herons, snowy and great egrets, and black-crowned night herons. Ospreys nest on large dead snags.

John Carlon stated: "We recognize that all of our projects—restoration, farming, and land acquisitions—have neighbors and affect communities. Our goal is to balance the basic requirements of wildlife populations with the safety, economic, and recreational needs of local citizens. At the end of the day it's about people, not just the land."

(River Partners has compiled its multi-pronged and innovative strategies for habitat restoration and published them in *California Riparian Habitat Restoration Handbook*, which serves as a textbook for others interested in restoring riparian habitat.)

Sacramento River Conservation Area Forum

With the importance being given to restoring riparian growth and allowing the river to meander more, the rights and wishes of property owners, farmers, and recreationists often come into play. One organization has been given cen-

tral responsibility for coordinating projects that affect these interests—the Sacramento River Conservation Area Forum (SRCAF).

The forum grew out of 1986 legislation that called for a management plan to protect, restore, and enhance fisheries and riparian habitat from Keswick Dam to the town of Verona, 222 miles in all—the "Conservation Area." To that end, SRCAF did the following: coordinated the removal of riprap at Woodson Bridge/ Kopta Slough; developed a "Sacramento River Public Access" website; developed a "Safe Harbor" agreement to provide assurances for land-owners; adopted a "Good Neighbor" policy that seeks to prevent or redress any harm or loss to private landowners or entities; and enhanced bank swallow habitat.

Such measures that include improving a small piece of river, working out an agreement to allay the concerns of landowners, or recapturing a modest slice of wildlife habitat represent the hard work of conservation. It is seldom easy to balance varied interests. Nonetheless, the overall goal of a healthy river requires that diverse groups reach some agreement on how better to make this happen.

Mountain lions require wide swaths of habitat. Their numbers have rebounded in the Sacramento Valley. Trish Carney.

Preserving Open Space

"Property is more than real estate for many landowners. It is a part of the family heritage, a legacy to be passed on to future generations."

—*Northern California*
Regional Land Trust

What can landowners do who want to hold their land despite a bleak financial outlook and taxes to pay—who don't want to sell the land for development, even for huge financial gains? One option is a conservation or agricultural easement, most often generated through the work of a land trust. In most cases a land trust will pay the landowner in return for the conservation easement established for the property. The owner, typically a rancher or farmer, continues to hold title to the land, which he or she can work on a sustainable basis. Rights are retained for tilling, harvesting timber and minerals, using and diverting water, and raising livestock. The title can be passed on to heirs, but the land can never be sold. It will remain undeveloped, usually as open space, which may or may not be open to the public for recreational activities.

In the Sacramento Valley, land trusts and conservation easements significantly contribute to open space preservation, often farmlands. It's ironic that orchards and fields which replaced riparian forests, woodlands, and grasslands are now highly valued in the face of expanding urbanization, housing tracts, and other paved uses—a different kind of riparian succession. Land trusts are playing a key role to save these forms of open space.

One notable conservation easement happened in Shasta County in 2002.

Fenwood Ranch

Nestled along the Sacramento River in southern Shasta County sits 2,242 acres of land, including two and one-half miles of prime river frontage and wild riparian forest. Beyond are rolling hills, blue oak woodlands, and sweeping meadows. Gracing the scene are 300- to 500-year-old valley oaks, majestic trees disappearing across California in the wake of urban sprawl. Wildlife is abundant, including special-status species like the bank swallow. The rare native wildflower, silky cryptantha, grows there, as do elderberry bushes (host for the valley elderberry longhorn beetle) and pipevines (host for the pipevine swallowtail butterfly). Cow Creek and Bear Creek, historical arteries for migrating salmon, flank the property on either side; vernal pools are sprinkled throughout the landscape.

The river in this area has no spectacular bends or rapids, yet its moving presence is compelling. If one stands or sits on its banks and listens, it will speak. Even when not seen or heard, it is a constant force.

This serene slice of nature—known as Fenwood Ranch—is also rich in human history. A well-preserved "pit" dwelling along a stream marks former Native American habitat. Artifacts reveal the presence of Hudson Bay trappers and other frontiersmen. Lurking about are remnants from the town of Parkville and a Chinese community that sold vegetables to locals in the gold rush era. The historic Nobles Trail rims the property. And when the Sacramento's currents were determined by seasonal rhythms and not dam releases, travelers crossed it there in wagons during low summer flows.

Fenwood Ranch is a working ranch. Longtime Shasta County ranchers Jim and Mary Rickert graze their organically certified Prather cows on the profuse grasses and clovers covering the expansive meadows. In spring and early summer these are usually carpeted by the native wildflower goldfields.

Remarkably, this land was once going to be covered by asphalt and buildings. In the 1990s, its Bay Area owner launched a grandiose plan to develop "Eagle River," a town encompassing 1,750 housing units, an elementary school, a 27-hole golf course, 6,000-square-foot swim and tennis club, an almost 10-acre equestrian center, 80-room hotel with marina, 100,000-square-foot business park, 80,000-square-foot commercial area, and sheriff and fire department facilities. The owner's house was to be perched on the highest rise. In 1998, to the dismay of many citizens, the county approved this project. Before work began, however, the owner suffered a heart attack and died.

The plans sat there, waiting for someone to buy and develop the property. The deceased owner's four grown children had little interest in the project, or even in Fenwood itself. But when they came to spread their father's ashes on the land, they concluded that it needed to be preserved.

At this same time, Jim Rickert, who was leasing the land to graze livestock, was also pondering the future of the bucolic setting he and his wife had come to love. He thought a conservation easement might apply here. The owners liked the idea. Rickert contacted the Shasta Land Trust (SLT), a fledgling organization looking for its first project. Founder and board chair Kathleen Gilman, supported by her board, seized the opportunity to preserve Fenwood. Mike Reeves of the Trust for Public Land provided counsel on how to proceed, and the two trusts partnered on the project. Grants allowed SLT to purchase a conservation easement for more than half the appraised fair market value of the property. The owners received this compensation, while the conservation easement ensured that its open space would always remain so. Beyond a home building site, there would be no new buildings, roads, tree harvesting, or any other human alterations, except for those required to add further protections.

With Fenwood's price now reduced, the owners asked the Rickerts if they might be interested in owning it. They were and subsequently bought the property. They continue to graze livestock there and try to sustain the ranch's natural features. They fenced off river and creek banks to keep cows from trampling them; they installed a solar-powered pump to maintain a well; they rotate grazing so the meadows can regenerate. Their son James, who manages the ranch, is restoring the property's historical "China Garden" area, which involves eliminating invasive plants and bringing back natives.

The Rickert family is happy to continue their livelihood at Fenwood while preserving for future generations "the way California used to be." Shasta Land Trust and the Trust for Public Land have protected in perpetuity a sublime piece of watershed that helps nurture the vital waterway coursing by Fenwood's banks, and in turn be nurtured by it. Shasta Land Trust

Meadow at Fenwood Ranch, a Shasta Land Trust conservation easement. Lassen Peak shows in the distance. Shasta Land Trust.

holds events at Fenwood so the public can enjoy and learn from the river, land, plants, and wildlife.

Still gathering dust in a drawer someplace are the plans and map of "Eagle River."

Rush Ranch

Another prime piece of natural habitat is Rush Ranch, located off Highway 12 on Grizzly Island Road in the Suisun marshlands. Here, Patwin Indians once lived. When European-Americans came, they established a few ranches in the area. Today it is a hunter's paradise, with approximately 158 duck clubs and a pheasant hunting preserve.

Only about ten square miles of the historical wetlands remain, perhaps the best brackish tidal marsh habitat left in the United States. Rush Ranch occupies one of those square miles. The Solano Land Trust—formerly the Solano County Farmlands and Open Space Foundation—purchased the ranch in 1988 with a grant from the Coastal Conservancy. Visitors can see Patwin and other historic structures, walk trails, and observe wildlife. Throughout the fall and winter migrating seasons waterfowl are abundant. Rush Ranch was designated part of the San Francisco Bay National Estuarine Research Reserve in 2003.

Llano Seco Rancho

Llano Seco Rancho in Butte County is one of the last intact Mexican Land Grant ranches in California. Owned by the Thieriot family since the 1850s, it is a mosaic of wetlands, agricultural lands, riparian forest, oak woodlands, and native grasslands, all supporting a diverse array of wildlife. In 2006, the Northern California Regional Land Trust purchased an agricultural conservation easement from owner Richard Thieriot, who wished to preserve the natural values of the rancho and its vast properties,

while maintaining his ranching and farming activities. The easement conserves the largest remaining stands of valley oak woodlands and grain fields on the Sacramento River floodplain. Annually the rancho sustains peak populations of five hundred thousand ducks and one hundred thousand geese, along with a variety of special-status species, including the giant garter snake, greater sandhill crane, bald eagle, and Swainson's hawk.

Natomas Basin and Elkhorn Basin

Land trusts have preserved parcels in the Natomas and Elkhorn basins, which straddle the Sacramento on the east and west sides, respectively. Before agriculture transformed them, these areas were once dominated by tule swamps and massive oak groves and served as prolific flood zones. In the early 1970s, Sacramento officials approved a massive housing project for Natomas Basin, twenty minutes from downtown Sacramento. The Sacramento Valley Conservancy formed and halted the project. A conservation easement preserved close to 7,500 acres. Farming continues on some of the land; the rest is kept as wildlife habitat. Much of this land still serves as a critical floodplain.

Across the river is the Elkhorn Basin, another area dominated by a vast floodplain—and rich in history. Elkhorn Ranch once grew hops for beer, before prohibition stifled it. Orchards and tomato and rice farming then took over. A ferry transported autos across the river until 1969 when the Vietnam Veterans Memorial Bridge over Interstate 5 was built. In 1988, the Yolo Land Trust was formed to preserve lands in Yolo County, including the Elkhorn Basin.

In a symbolic "bridge" across the Sacramento River, the Sacramento Valley Conservancy and Yolo Land Trust combined in 2008 to purchase Elkhorn Ranch, linking the two counties in this preservation effort.

The Upper Sac was one of the richest waterways and rainbow trout fisheries in the country. One event changed everything. Craig Nielsen.

Conservation on the Upper Sac

Throughout the second half of the twentieth century, while the lower river was getting buffeted by water demands and increased flood protections, the Upper Sac also saw changes. The first major one came in 1969 when a dam was placed at the head of Box Canyon to collect the numerous headwater streams above the canyon. The new impoundment was called Lake Siskiyou. It is reportedly the only reservoir in California built primarily for recreation, although flood protection is often cited as a reason. The river below the dam is controlled through releases in a "run-of-the-river" mode that attempts to mimic natural flows.

Forty miles downriver from Box Canyon Dam is Shasta Lake and Shasta Dam, which ended salmon and steelhead runs above it. Nonetheless, the wild rainbow trout fishery in the Upper Sac remained robust, augmented by annual stocking of tens of thousands of hatchery trout. According to journalist Larry Green, who reported about Northern California fishing in the 1970s and '80s, the fishery of the Upper Sac was a "never-ending resource.... Acre for acre, this river holds greater numbers of trout than any I can name."

Green was right about the abundance of

rainbow trout but wrong about it being a never-ending resource. On July 14, 1991, a devastating event virtually wiped out the fishery overnight. Shortly before 10 P.M., a train derailed on a bridge along the sharp bend known as the Cantara Loop just north of Dunsmuir—the same severe roundabout that tested builders in

at least nineteen thousand gallons into the swift-moving river.

Early the next morning, people reported a foul odor and burning eyes. Dunsmuir residents became ill with dizziness, vomiting, rashes, headaches, and respiratory problems. Many evacuated the town. By noon the Cali-

On July 14, 1991, a train toppled from the tracks on the infamous Cantara Loop, dumping poisonous metham sodium into the river. Record Searchlight.

the late 1880s and locomotive engineers ever since. In the fifteen years before 1991, thirty-six derailments reportedly happened there. But none produced the immense damage of the one in 1991, when several rail cars slipped off the track bed and toppled into the river. One carried a potent pesticide containing metham sodium, a chemical used to control or kill weeds, soil diseases, nematodes, and insects. The car ruptured at 9:50 P.M. and slowly leaked

fornia Highway Patrol closed a major highway along the river due to drivers experiencing discomfort from fumes. The river carried the light yellow-green plume all the way to Shasta Lake. Wherever it flowed it killed organisms almost instantly. Thousands of dead trout and other species floated to the surface, collected along the shore, in eddies, against brush and rocks, and sank back down to pool bottoms. Foliage bordering the river quickly started turning brown.

The plume of metham sodium from the July 14, 1991, spill flowed down the river all the way to Shasta Lake. California Department of Fish and Game.

The metham sodium plume killed fish and most other organisms along its deadly course. California Department of Fish and Game.

In two weeks the contaminant had dissipated, but the damage had been done. One million fish, including 300,000 trout and 650,000 riffle sculpin, thousands of crayfish, snails, clams, and Pacific giant salamanders, plus millions of insects, were killed. Tens of thousands of willows, alders, and cottonwoods eventually died; many others were severely weakened. The riparian canopy cover was wiped out, leading to a further loss of wildlife, such as birds, otters, bats, and mink.

Dunsmuir and other communities, and especially businesses that catered to recreation, were devastated. Many citizens pushed hard to quickly restock the river with hatchery-reared fish.

Two members of the DFG office in Redding, wild trout biologist Mike Berry and district biologist Mike Rode, were the first officials on the scene of the derailment. In studying the situation, they concluded that stocking hatchery fish would actually impede the river's recovery. Invertebrates—the bottom of the aquatic food chain—first needed to repopulate the water. If trout—the top of the food chain—were initially dumped into the water, they would devour whatever invertebrate life started coming back, thereby indefinitely preventing a full recovery. Plus, a massive influx of hatchery-bred rainbow trout could interbreed with wild rainbows and create a population of hybridized fish, compromising the genetic purity and strength of the native fish. In their view, the long-term health of the river and fishery trumped short-term interests.

Berry and Rode urged a "bottom-up" ecological approach that allowed the river to recover naturally. They believed enough wild trout were still left in the hundreds of miles of tributaries feeding the Upper Sac to re-colonize the river. To their thinking, the disaster presented an opportunity to not only restore the river's

DFG biologist Mike Berry. Department of Fish and Game

wild trout fishery but possibly make it stronger. The fisheries branch chief in the Sacramento DFG office, Tim Farley, agreed. He decided not to stock the river, gambling that Berry and Rode's analysis was correct.

Soon after the chemical spill, the "money spill" followed. The Southern Pacific Railroad Company, anxious to head off lawsuits, sent lawyers to Dunsmuir to try to settle with individuals and businesses harmed by the incident. The company presented a till of $500,000 to reimburse injured parties. Some citizens sought and received compensation, others declined in favor of filing a class-action suit. This divided the community, already fractured over impacts of the catastrophe and who was to blame. Given that Dunsmuir was a railroad town, residents were reluctant to hold Southern Pacific totally responsible, preferring to settle with the company without going to court.

Confusion over responsibility quickly surfaced. Amazingly, metham sodium was not classified as a "marine pollutant" at the time, so as one representative for the state Public Utilities Commission put it: "Because we did not initially believe we had a hazardous material involved in the derailment, we did not react to this as we would have if someone had called and said we have a chlorine tank leaking, for example." Southern Pacific also believed it could have acted more swiftly to get the rail car out of the river, were it not for the overlapping jurisdictions of government agencies, each of which had to approve any action. Southern Pacific and the Public Utilities Commission also weren't entirely sure who had responsibility for the river (they later wound up suing each other). So the car stayed put, until it had fully emptied.

Joined by the federal government, the State of California filed its own lawsuit, arguing that the river and its fish belong to the public. The judgment in favor of the plaintiffs amounted to $38 million. Southern Pacific had to pay $32 million, with other responsible entities, like the rail car and chemical manufacturers, providing another $6 million. Approximately $21 million went for damages, reimbursements, restoration, and other costs. Fourteen million was used to establish the Cantara Trustee Council to help guide recovery efforts. Although there were some restoration projects on the river itself, the bulk of funds went to habitat acquisition and resource enhancement in other watersheds, study and research, and education. Restoration of the Upper Sac would largely occur naturally.

A citizens group was formed to help bring the splintered community together. The Cantara Trustee Council funded the Upper Sacramento River Exchange (later shortened to the River Exchange). A "River Center" was created for meetings and discussions of such highly contentious issues as money, assigning blame, and restoring fishing and businesses. Leading

Diane Strachan (right) conducting a workshop. Provided by Diane Strachan.

this effort was Diane Strachan, a founder and first executive director of the River Exchange.

From these efforts and Strachan's effective facilitation, citizens began to refocus their energies on the river's importance to the community. The need to educate people about the fragility of a river and its vital ecology became the exchange's priority. The group hired Vince Cloward, a former school teacher, to organize and lead activities advancing education and river stewardship. Cloward reported that over time, community divisiveness slowly dissipated, replaced by a spirit of collaboration that rallied around the river's well-being.

As important as disbursement of funds and community healing was, the mainstay of the Upper Sac and its communities has always been

One of many railroad bridges crossing the Sacramento River. This one is in Redding. Bob Madgic.

trout fishing. DFG official Steve Turek led the fishery restoration effort. The DFG and California Fish and Game Commission imposed a total ban on angling in the entire Upper Sac for three years to allow native fauna and flora to recover. As difficult as this was for residents, the decision not to plant the river immediately with hatchery stock proved correct. Wild rainbows repopulated the waters much sooner than anyone had hoped, and in three years the river reopened to fishing. To create recreational angling for locals, the DFG planted hatchery fish in a six-mile stretch in and around Dunsmuir. The rest of the river was strictly for wild trout, with a two-trout limit.

Today, the Upper Sac once again is a world-class wild rainbow trout fishery.

~

With stunning perspicacity, Thomas Jefferson long ago spoke: "In the environment, every victory is temporary, every defeat permanent."

Jefferson's statement declares that ongoing human efforts are required to protect the earth.

Or, as Wallace Stegner wrote, "Environmentalism or conservation or preservation, or whatever it should be called, is not a fact, and never has been. It is a job."

And it's a tough job. It requires engaging in the messy political arena where conflicting interests prevail; seeking to get laws passed and followed; writing grants and raising money; hammering out agreements among differing parties; convincing others that future benefits are more important than short-term returns; educating people on ecology so they see that the survival of a beetle has implications for humankind. It is a never-ending process.

Fortunately for the health of the planet, countless individuals and organizations have made this their unwavering mission. The attention given to the Sacramento River, in all its fragmented tapestry, demonstrates that these efforts pay off. The river meanders more freely; riparian vegetation grows again; open space remains; endangered species survive; and humans are learning to embrace nature's wisdom.

When flows are low, the fly fisher can find many places to wade on the Lower Sac. Bob Madgic.

CHAPTER TEN

River for Recreation and Contemplation

"Many men go fishing all of their lives without knowing that it is not fish they are after."

—*Henry David Thoreau*

A S RIVERS GO, THE SACRAMENTO OFFERS unparalleled recreational and personal growth opportunities. It invites visitors to drift down in a boat; greet the sunrise in a duck blind; walk briskly or ride a horse along its shores; paddle a canoe in the current; raft down gushing rapids; scream across the surface in a jet boat; or simply sit on a bank and reflect.

The river beckons one to join in and participate. Observe wildlife. Absorb the avian brilliance. Take a pathway and absorb energy from the nearby currents. Probe the waters with bait, lure, or fly. Hunt the game. Learn from the river, work to protect it. Or just enjoy it and allow its many gifts to replenish and restore.

Fishing

Whatever anglers seek, they can probably find it in the Sacramento River from below Shasta Dam all the way to the Delta. Beyond its rich endowment of native fish, the river contains a host of introduced species that have become more entrenched and abundant than anyone expected. These include American shad, striped bass, largemouth bass, and catfish.

First, the river from Redding to Red Bluff, referred to as the "Lower Sac."

Cold-Water Fishery

The Sacramento has long been the premier water in California for Chinook salmon. When runs are healthy, thousands of anglers seek to hook one of these kings of the fishing realm. Not only is hooking a salmon a rush, but anglers love to bring them home to eat. Salmon can be caught legally in the Sacramento from the Delta up to the Deschutes Bridge in Anderson.

Since migrating salmon don't feed, the angler's challenge is to provoke or entice one to take something in its mouth, such as an artificial lure or salmon roe. One strategy is to run lures past them that resemble small fish. For whatever instinctual reason, salmon will sometimes strike the lure. Another is to place a glob of salmon roe (usually cured with borox and hardened for months beforehand) on the hook and gently lift or bounce it periodically off the bottom. In order to spice up their roe, fishing guides often create their own "secret" formulas, by adding flesh or scent from crawdads, grass shrimp, anchovy, or some other enticer. Although it is puzzling why, salmon will often gently engulf roe in their mouths. One feels or senses the "take" and jerks the rod upwards, hoping a salmon is on the end of the line.

One of the most popular salmon fishing spots is the Barge Hole, near the mouth of Battle Creek. Allan Craig.

Salmon will also sometimes take an artificial fly, such as a small nymph pattern, which resembles the staple food of trout. Since salmon presumably don't consume such insects, why they will take an imitation bug as trout do is another mystery.

Beyond their recreational value, salmon deliver income. Commercial and recreational fishing for salmon, and its migrating companion steelhead, generate approximately $28.8 million to $50.6 million annually for the California economy. Until numbers of salmon declined in the 2000s, it's been a growing industry. Thirty to forty years ago, fishing guides on the Sacramento numbered perhaps thirty to thirty-five. By the end of the 1990s, there were more than 160. Some guides can make $60,000 to $70,000 a year, working six months. They in turn need tackle, and their jet boats require gas. One study concluded each salmon caught was worth $900 to $1,200 to the local economy; this breakdown included motel owners, restaurants, waiters, cooks, gas station owners, fishing shops, and more. A fishing store owner in Redding said he annually netted $75,000 during good salmon years.

Correspondingly, the drop in salmon runs that precipitated a fishing shutdown in 2008 and 2009 had a devastating effect on many livelihoods, with thousands of lost jobs and millions in lost income.

Another prized sport fish is the sea-run rain-

This lucky angler displays his catch of a Chinook salmon. Bob Madgic.

bow called steelhead. The Sacramento River was never a prime steelhead river like the Klamath, Trinity, or Smith, nor is it today with less than two thousand fish returning most years. Ninety percent of these are reared in the Coleman National Fish Hatchery. Such hatchery stock have their adipose fin clipped so officials and anglers can identify them. If the fin is not clipped, it's difficult to tell if a large rainbow is a resident wild trout or steelhead. Only laboratory testing that detects the presence of the ocean mineral strontium in the otolith (inner ear) bone can tell for sure whether the fish has been in salt water. If so, they are steelhead. There is some speculation that conditions are so good for trout in the Sacramento that they have

been content to stay put and not head out for the sea, thus accounting for the low numbers of steelhead.

The Lower Sac also holds a world-class rainbow trout fishery. In contrast to the mostly hatchery-reared salmon and steelhead, all the rainbow trout are wild. Ironically, what nurtured this special fishery was Shasta Dam. Although the dam blocked salmon and steelhead runs, it created "tailwaters"—river stretches dependent on dam releases for their flows. With Shasta in place, summer releases are usually maintained at flows of 12,000 to 14,000 cubic feet per second (cfs) to provide water for crops. These consistently colder flows also grow rainbow trout.

The emerging rainbow trout fishery was a local secret at first. One longtime Redding resident says he began catching healthy numbers of rainbows in the 1960s, often during his lunch break. Clear, cold water and strong currents spurred massive caddis and mayfly hatches. By the 1990s, the average-sized fish caught was sixteen inches, and fish over five pounds were common. The rainbows were a mix of native strains from varied tributaries, creating a robust population of resilient fish and a fly fisher's nirvana.

The rainbow population at first seemed to dissipate below Anderson where the river warmed. But when a temperature control device was placed at Shasta Dam in 1997 to help salmon, the colder water kept extending farther downriver. Soon, rainbows were being caught beyond Red Bluff.

The Sacramento is big as trout waters go. An angler should see it as a composite of small streams and fish these accordingly, whether from a drift boat or by wading. A boat allows one to fish more water, often ten miles in a day's drift. But some anglers prefer fishing a few stretches repeatedly, becoming intimate with their particular idiosyncrasies, moods, mysteries, and rewards.

The fly fisher seeks this immersion in the world of the trout. He or she drifts with the current in a boat, or stands in the flowing water with its force pushing against his or her legs. An artificial fly is at the end of the line, perhaps one he tied himself. He is trying to connect with the trout—where they lie, what they eat, and what drives their actions. When a trout selects an imitation fly out of thousands of real insects, it is not a "catch" as much as a joining. The fly fisher can feel the throbbing of the trout; in turn, the fish is responding to the force emanating from the line. This connection, this link between human and fish in this natural realm, can be, for some, a Zen-like experience. As someone said, fishing is time-consuming, but that's the point.

And when one holds a beautiful Sacramento rainbow trout, returning it to the water seems exactly right. Most anglers practice "catch and release" with these treasured wild rainbows; it is not food they are after. Roderick Haig-Brown,

Mike Michalak, river steward and owner of The Fly Shop in Redding. Courtesy of The Fly Shop.

A Sacramento River rainbow trout, soon to be released back into the river. Allan Craig.

A fly fisher and a deer share the river. For success in fishing, the angler should see the Sacramento as a composite of smaller rivulets. Bob Madgic.

preeminent writer on rivers and fly fishing, described the sport's origin this way: "Our tradition is that of the first man who sneaked away to the creek when the tribe did not really need fish."

In doing so, he discovered what Thoreau and millions of anglers have learned in their quests to hook fish.

Warm-Water Fishery

From Red Bluff to the Sacramento-San Joaquin Delta estuary is 150 miles of fishable water. The Delta contains the greatest abundance of prized game and food fish, mostly introduced species.

One native warm-water game fish is the behemoth white sturgeon. (The native green sturgeon is a threatened species and off limits to fishing.) Brian Doyle, fascinated with ancient sturgeon in the Columbia River, wrote in *Orion* magazine: "The fact there are wild creatures bigger and heavier than cars right there in the river…is astounding. Seeing one of these 'dinosaurs' grants us humility."

At one time, market fishermen targeted white sturgeon for their eggs, which are made into caviar, and their tasty white flesh. In the 1880s, several hundred thousand pounds of these fish were caught annually in California. Each fish represented decades of life. Such depletion—similar to the harvesting of ancient redwoods—was accompanied by habitat degradation and almost caused sturgeon to disappear. In 1917, authorities closed the fishery. It reopened in 1954 for sport fishing and with tight restric-

The Delta requires a boat for most angling. Bill Wells.

tions. The species bounced back, only to crash again in 2006 to a meager ten thousand adults. Crackdowns on illegal poaching and stringent angling regulations are helping bring back the sturgeon populations.

Sturgeon are opportunistic bottom feeders. Four rubbery whiskers, or feelers, front a small, funnel-like mouth on the underside of the head. When feeding, the fish roots in the mud and uses its sensitive whiskers to locate food. It then sucks up whatever edible and often foreign materials it uncovers.

For bait, anglers use clams, crabs, grass shrimp, sardines, blood worms, and pile worms,

among other foods. Angling regulations require the release of all sturgeon under forty-six inches and over sixty-six inches. A fisherman can only keep one per day and three per year. Such regulations are helping to restore sturgeon populations, though they are still far from their historic numbers.

Beyond sturgeon, and migrating salmon and steelhead, all other fishing in the lower river and Delta is for exotic species. Among the scrappiest are imports from the Atlantic Ocean: American shad and striped bass. Although shad typically weigh one to three pounds, and seldom exceed six pounds, they are exceptionally strong fighters. They migrate in bunches, so once located they can provide continuous angling action.

Striped bass also run in schools. Unlike most other fish, they spawn on the surface. Highly predatory, stripers will eat just about any fish their mouth can grasp. They can quickly deplete a school of bait fish like threadfin shad. So anglers use lures or jigs or streamer fly patterns

rotten pieces of meat. The angler places bait on or near the bottom and waits for a catfish to swallow it. Catfish typically weigh in at a pound or two, but some tip the scales at eight to ten pounds, and occasionally weigh more than twenty pounds.

Thousands of pounds of catfish were once netted each year for the market, but this is no longer allowed. Today many "fish farms" raise

Striped bass are a prized sport fish in the lower river and Delta. Dan Frost.

resembling small fish and regularly catch eight- to twenty-pounders. Stripers reared in the bay, as distinct from those raised in a hatchery, can reach fifty pounds.

Other introduced species popular with anglers are in the sunfish and catfish families. Few beginning fishing experiences surpass seeing a bobber going up and down from a bluegill feeding on a worm, bug, or fish egg.

According to some, catfish are the most dependable and best eating fish in the Delta. The three most common species are bullhead, white catfish, and channel catfish. These fish lie low and deep, and feed mainly at night. Non-discriminating feeders, they take bait like clams, anchovies, nightcrawlers, dough baits, sardines, chicken or turkey livers, bloodworms, and even

catfish and sell them, and several valley eating establishments regularly offer a "catfish fry."

The only remaining commercial market in Sacramento waters is for crawdads, also called crayfish, a lobster-like crustacean usually under eight inches. The two Delta species are the red swamp crayfish and the signal crayfish, both invasive pests that have replaced the native sooty crawdad and threaten the ecology in unknown ways. (The only remaining native crawdad species in California is the endangered Shasta crawdad, found in Shasta County.) Being night feeders, they are best caught in baited traps—perforated cans of cheap dog food work well—left overnight. There is no limit or season on these tasty creatures.

The most popular gamefish in America is

black bass, also called largemouth bass, and it, too, lurks in Delta waters. After being introduced to California in the early 1900s, this species quickly became an angling favorite. Aggressive feeders and tenacious fighters, black bass will viciously attack anything resembling food, including small fish, frogs, snakes, mice, even small birds. They love weedy shorelines where their target foods hang out.

Bobby Barrack is one of the region's long-time fishing guides. His family has lived along the Delta since the 1950s. He relates: "I guide over 100 days a year, and in order to consistently get hookups for my clients, I have to solve the puzzles presented by constantly changing water levels and tides, different structures where fish hang out, and differing fish temperaments depending on weather and season. I love the challenge of trying to crack the code each time out."

Fishing for each of these outstanding game fish has led to the highly popular fishing tour-

Fishing guide and tournament competitor Bobby Barrack displays prize-winning catch of a largemouth bass. Stacy Barrack.

A father instructing his son in fishing techniques. Bob Madgic.

nament, where anglers compete to see who can catch the most pounds of fish, or the largest, or some other measure. Cash prizes usually start at $1,000. At Shasta Lake, for instance, "fishing derbies" for either trout or bass are annual events. But nothing compares to the Delta for number of tournaments, including ones for sturgeon, striped bass, and black bass. To protect breeding stock, which are normally the largest fish, competitions for sturgeon and striped bass feature a "target length" as decided by the spin of a wheel. The angler who catches a fish closest to that length without going over it is the winner.

Black-bass competitions reign supreme in the Delta, which boasts the highest total weight of catches and most black-bass tournaments in the world. The three-day Rio Vista Bass Derby typically swells the town's population from five thousand to thirty-five thousand. For the bigger tournaments, hundreds of anglers come from across the country, competing either singly or in teams for prizes up to $100,000 that sometimes include a boat. The fish are kept in water containers for measurement, and then released.

~

For some, fishing is mainly about serenity, solitude, and conjoining with nature. For others, it's a frantic contest for hookups—a test of fishing prowess and outlet for competitive urges. Regardless, it's the connection with one of the Sacramento's prized underwater specimens that at first draws the angler, who surely discovers the ample rewards that lay beyond, whatever they may be.

Hunting

Thoreau's insight into the world of fishing might also apply to hunting. Here the past is considerably more checkered, however, as unbridled killings once dominated the landscape.

Two hundred years ago California teemed with game. Vast herds of elk and antelope, countless deer and black and grizzly bears roamed the Central Valley and foothills. Cougar, lynx, bobcat, fox, wolves, and coyotes prowled the landscapes stalking prey. Birds of all sizes and colors were everywhere. The native people revered such natural bounty. They killed only what they could eat.

European newcomers consumed many of the mammals and birds they shot. But they also killed for sport and "entertainment." Spanish and Mexican rancheros and vaqueros delighted in lassoing and killing bears that came at night to feast on slaughtered cattle. Elk received the same treatment. The Americanos were little different. Soldiers in San Francisco's Presidio, for example, reportedly roped and killed forty bears in one night, just for fun. Horsemen ran pronghorn antelope to exhaustion before shooting them. "Great sport" is how one put it. Later settlers staged infamous, fight-to-the-death matches between bulls and grizzlies.

The gold rush heightened the killing. Miners flocking to the Golden State showed little restraint in shooting whatever crossed their paths or lurked nearby.

The commercialization of hunting (and fishing) spurred such rampant killings. All types of mammals and birds were systematically slaughtered. The meat and sometimes fur, plumage, and body parts were sold to national and international markets. As the country became more populated, the government itself tried to exterminate animal pests and predators. States offered bounties. In as 1931, Congress passed an Animal Damage Control Act that legitimized "the destruction of mountain lions, coyotes, bobcats, prairie dogs, gophers, ground squirrels, jackrabbits, and other animals injurious to agriculture, horticulture, forestry, husbandry, game, or domestic animals, or that carried disease." Federal authorities killed (numbers are surely understated) some 26,000 bears, 500,000 bobcats, 50,000 red wolves, 1,600 gray wolves, 8,000 mountain lions, and millions of coyotes throughout the country between 1937 and 1983. The act remains in place today.

All this slaughter exacted a harsh toll. The last California grizzly was shot in 1922. Wolves, never that numerous in California, were wiped out. Few antelope survived. The immense herds of tule elk that one observer noted "darkened the plain for miles and looked like great herds of cattle in the distance," were reduced to single digits. These few were fortunately placed in refuges, and today the tule elk population numbers between 3,500 and 4,000.

Nothing rivaled birds in sheer numbers. The Pacific Flyway brought in millions of snow geese, Canada geese, and white-fronted geese to the Sacramento Valley, there joined by a myriad of duck species. One observer near Suisun Bay in the mid-1800s reported seeing a flight of geese about "100 yards wide, flying in a seemingly endless stream from over the western hills," darkening the sky for almost twenty minutes. These and other game birds like grouse, sage hens, prairie chickens, quail, partridge, doves, and wild pigeons, attracted shooters by the score. Behind the killing rampages were desperate farmers and market hunters who supplied urban markets with fowl (chicken and turkey farms were largely non-existent at this time).

Geese and ducks had long decimated agricultural fields. Farmers or hired lackeys blasted away with guns, even rockets, to disperse or kill them. So many waterfowl were being slaughtered each year that some feared species would disappear, like the passenger pigeon did.

To halt the carnage, the Migratory Bird Treaty Act was passed in 1918. It prohibited the commercial killing of birds migrating between Canada and the United States, while also stipulating how, when, and where birds could be hunted. (Similar conventions with other countries followed.)

This law was basically ignored and unenforced for decades. A few sheriffs and judges were market hunters themselves. It fell to a small contingent of game wardens to police the entire Sacramento Valley. One was Terry Grosz. He earned bachelor and master of science degrees in wildlife management from Humboldt State University and, soon after leaving college in 1966, became a game warden.

Grosz began aggressively enforcing the laws. His life's mission was to save waterfowl. He often worked eighteen-hour days, seven days a week. He would lie in wait—creeping and hiding sometimes all night in mud and tules—to surprise law-breakers. When he once observed three "draggers"—so-called because they killed so many birds they had to tie them in bundles and drag them away—"blowing up" ducks by the hundreds, he waited (for his own safety) until they dropped their guns before moving in to arrest them. A fourth man hidden nearby shot Grosz three times in the back with shotgun blasts. Grosz's wounds were temporarily debilitating but not life-threatening. It was one of six attempts on his life throughout his career.

Across a decade, Grosz caught over ten thousand lawbreakers, prosecuted all but six, sent many to prison, and collected over $1 million dollars in fines.

In retirement Grosz authored several books about his times as an officer, including *Slaughter in the Sacramento Valley*. He quotes one market hunter: "I know myself and others like me are not totally responsible for the loss of waterfowl in the Sacramento Valley today, but I would bet we had a lot to do with it. God will have to create another earth like this one before we see such wonders like the great clouds of ducks and geese I saw of old. I will never ever kill another duck again as long as I live."

The Highs and Lows of Being a Warden

TERRY GROSZ says a high point in his career came when he finally arrested an individual named "Joe" who told Grosz that he was "so stupid that you could never catch me. You have walked within feet of where I was hiding more than a dozen times." Grosz knew this man was one of the worst violators in the valley, but he couldn't catch him in the act. In a strange bargain Joe agreed to teach Grosz the methods market hunters used to elude the law. The 71-year-old informer figured that the more men Grosz arrested, the less competition he would have. Using this information, the warden did indeed catch several violators. But he still had his sights set on Joe.

The next season Grosz was near the Delevan Wildlife Refuge, off-limits to hunting. At 3 A.M. he heard deafening shotgun blasts and the raucous clamor of fleeing ducks. In due time, tied bundles of dead pintail ducks came floating down the nearby canal and into a pond behind a small dam. Grosz waited in the bushes. Still before sunrise, Joe showed up to gather his booty. When Grosz confronted him, Joe merely asked the warden to help him stuff the ducks in a gunnysack. Grosz took him home, fed him breakfast, and cited him for six violations: early shooting of waterfowl (before dawn); illegal shotgun (ability to fire multiple shells); no hunting license in possession; killing ducks over limit; no federal duck stamp; and hunting on a closed wildlife refuge. Each violation was $500.

The following Monday, Joe showed up on Grosz's doorstep, shotgun in hand, causing Grosz to fear he was going to get shot. But the man started crying, gave the shotgun to Grosz, and said, "I'm all done." Apparently Joe was so ashamed to have gotten caught that he stopped killing ducks from that point on.

When asked what his low point was as a warden, Grosz replied: "I loved the ducks and wanted to see this resource be there in the future, but I just couldn't get the job done. I couldn't stop the killing."

Grosz retired in 1998. In 2002 he was awarded an honorary doctorate degree by Unity College in Maine for "Environmental Stewardship."

Sacramento Valley Hunting Today

Beyond the wanton slaughter of wildlife, hunting opportunities in the Sacramento Valley have been severely diminished with the loss of riparian forests and wetlands. Where habitat still exists, deer and many smaller mammals are still widely hunted. Several introduced species now popular as prey include wild boar, first imported from Europe and Asia; the ring-necked pheasant from Asia; and wild turkey, an import from the southeastern United States.

The major hunting in the Sacramento Valley is for birds. Although the numbers of migratory and resident waterfowl don't rival the historic tens of millions, wildlife refuges, rice fields, and private lands have helped restore respectable numbers. For example, the valley accommodates approximately 2.3 million ducks per year on average; 1.5 million geese; 220,000 coots; 50,000 to 100,000 trumpeter swans; and 10,000 to 20,000 sandhill cranes.

Except for predatory species, California officials have long sought to protect its wild heritage. A State Board of Fish Commissioners, first established in 1870, set seasons and legal hunting methods. A Division of Fish and Game followed in 1927, to be replaced in 1951 with the Department of Fish and Game. Its mission was (and remains) one of "managing fish, wildlife and plant resources for their ecological values and for their use and enjoyment by the public." But by this time California's wild creatures had

Duck hunting at first light. Chadd Santerre.

A good retriever dog is often a hunter's best companion and aide. Chadd Santerre.

been decimated, and its wild places were disappearing. Conservationists and hunters led the charge to preserve what remained.

Hunters are often called "the first conservationists." Many of them have long upheld the ethics of their sport and are deeply grounded in a kinship with nature. Author David Petersen writes: "Hunting is by nature and tradition a back-to-basics endeavor, a ceremony of process over product, a celebration of our evolved human-animal wildness tempered by respect for all living things, by conscious self-restraint (that's the 'sport' part), and founded in personal honor when no one else is watching."

Most ethical hunters consume what they kill. Families today still rely on game to augment their food supply. Petersen states: "Compared to factory farming, ethical hunting is a truly benign and honorable—not to mention healthy—way to get your meat."

To sustain their sport, hunters formed organizations to preserve and restore habitat. These organizations include California Waterfowl Association, Ducks Unlimited, Wilderness Unlimited, California Deer Association, Rocky Mountain Elk Foundation, and many private hunting clubs.

Today more hunting is being done on private lands than ever before. Some groups provide financial incentives for landowners to open their lands for hunting and fishing. Wilderness Unlimited, for example, leases or buys lands outright for use by its members.

Ducks Unlimited, the world's largest nonprofit organization dedicated to conserving North America's disappearing waterfowl habitats, works with rice farmers to build fish-safe water diversions from the Sacramento River and to sustain flooded rice fields, a key waterfowl habitat.

The California Waterfowl Association has an active youth education program and involves youth in many "hands-on" activities. Chadd Santerre.

California Waterfowl Association member instructing youngster on firearms. Chadd Santerre.

The Yolo Wildlife Area near Sacramento is popular with birders and hunters. Dave Feliz.

By 2011, the California Waterfowl Association had completed over 875 projects that protected, restored, and enhanced in excess of 400,000 acres of wetlands. Its wood duck program has hatched almost 600,000 ducklings; banding programs have marked more than 185,000 waterfowl; and youth and education programs have reached more than 250,000 people.

The Rocky Mountain Elk Foundation is dedicated to preserving elk habitat. California is the only state with three elk species: tule elk (population 3,500 to 4,000), Roosevelt elk 3,500), and Rocky Mountain elk (1,500).

Remarkably, tule elk can once again be hunted, primarily in Grizzly Island Wildlife Area, where a sustainable herd exists. This California wildlife area is part of the Great Suisun Marsh, which at 84,000 acres is the largest estuarine marsh in America. Grizzly occupies 15,300 acres, some sitting below sea level. The

DFG constructs and maintains levees and other facilities that enhance public recreational use. It plants barley on more than two thousand acres to feed migrating birds.

It's somewhat anomalous that hunting occurs in state and federal wildlife areas and refuges devoted to restoring habitat and wildlife. Public hunting is permitted, for instance, on portions of the Sacramento, Delevan, Colusa, Sutter, and Sacramento River national wildlife refuges. It's also available on other public lands along the river corridor if not prohibited by city ordinances and not within 150 yards of any occupied or functional building.

One prime public hunting and recreational area is the Vic Fazio Yolo Wildlife Area, located in the Yolo Basin where the Sacramento River makes a sweeping bend between Sacramento and Woodland. At 16,000-plus acres, the basin is the largest public/private restoration project west of the Florida Everglades. During fall and

U.S. Fish & Wildlife biologist Joe Silveira monitors Sacramento Valley wildlife and educates the public about it. U.S. Fish & Wildlife Service.

winter, hunters can hunt for birds within sight of Sacramento skyscrapers.

To sustain the resource, the DFG allows hunters to harvest waterfowl at levels below normal reductions from disease and other environmental factors—a formula called "compensatory mortality." According to U.S. Fish and Wildlife biologist Joseph Silveira, healthy populations of waterfowl can be maintained or even increased if the hunting harvest does not exceed the rate of natural mortality. He says this is why breeding surveys and banding efforts are so important—they yield information about population sizes and age- and sex-related mortalities that help wildlife managers.

History reveals the abominable practices pursued against wildlife, most of it totally deviant from those of the true sportsman. Today, hunting organizations and hunter-conservationists are committed to sustaining wildlife. Chadd Santerre, wildlife biologist for the California Waterfowl Association, says, "Hunting and conservation are intimately connected. Too many people don't understand that pavement

and concrete remove wildlife forever. The hunter quickly learns this."

One of the nation's most renowned hunters and sportsmen probably stated it best: "The wildlife of today is not ours to do with as we please. The original stock was given to us in trust for the benefit of the present and the future. We must render an accounting of this trust to those who come after us."

So spoke Theodore Roosevelt.

Boating

Rivers historically provided a means for humans to get from place to place. Beyond this utility, people have long reveled in skimming across water in some kind of craft. On the Sacramento, engine-powered jet boats, speedboats, Jet Skis, and the like all churn the river's waters for recreation.

One kind of motorized boating—houseboating—wants quiet waters, like Shasta Lake, Trinity Lake, Oroville Lake, and the Delta. Literally a getaway lodge on water, a houseboat offers a place to eat, relax, and sleep, as well as engage in water sports. In the Delta, the

All kinds of motorized boats ply the Sacramento's waters. Bob Madgic.

seemingly endless channels and sloughs—a thousand miles of inland rivulets dotted with islands—invite solitude. A 360-degree view captures the snowy peaks of the Sierra Nevada around to the Coast Range, with imposing Mt. Diablo standing due west like a sentry. Some houseboaters tie up to a tree or some other snag, a practice called "gunk-holing," and settle in. Life slows to what is called "Delta time."

Some boaters prefer more engaging activity, such as canoeing, kayaking, and rafting. The current grips and transports the boater at its own pace. Being part of such a natural force is rapturous, spawning the contentment of "going with the flow." Such force is usually tempered with an oar or paddle—muscle power rather than machine power—accentuating one's connection with nature.

The Upper Sacramento offers fast-paced action, especially for rafters and kayakers during spring runoff. The rafting run from Box Canyon to Shasta Lake is rated Class II to III on the international river-runner's scale (Class I is flat moving water; Class VI is life-threatening rapids). The gradient drops fifty-seven feet per mile. (The steeper the gradient, the more the river "drops," meaning more whitewater and severe rapids.)

The Lower Sac, by comparison, runs at a gradient of less than ten feet per mile and is generally rated a Class II run. Although rapids are infrequent, the current is swift and strong, averaging five miles or more an hour. The Bureau of Reclamation's water releases from Shasta and Keswick dams determine flow levels. A smooth expanse can be transformed into a level II rapid when lower flows bring rocks closer to the surface. Higher flows can create gushing turbulence and class II or even III rapids. Strong currents, hydraulics (reversals, crosscurrents), and

Many kayakers go downriver, fewer paddle upriver. Bob Madgic.

Canine canoe mates. Bob Madgic.

Houseboating and angling are both popular in the Delta, often in the fog. Bill Corps.

College students take to the river with float tubes each year on Labor Day. Bruce King.

obstacles (trees, bushes, rocks) can cause even the most stable boats to flip. During flood conditions—dam releases of 50,000 cfs or more—the river becomes too dangerous for any craft.

To guide a craft through turbulent currents and rapids, one must learn to "read the water"—knowing where its power resides and the direction and force of its many tongues, shoots, and glides—and work in harmony with it. If the bow doesn't slice into the current directly, a powerful side force can topple a craft.

On any given day, one can see kayakers, canoeists, or rafters riding the currents downriver. Sometimes a dozen or more such crafts streak the river with bright colors and patterns. Those loaded with gear imply an overnight journey, with camping along the shore. During brutally hot summer days, some may choose a float tube or spongy raft to seek the river's cooling gifts.

During the summer, North County Raft Rental Company of Redding schedules as many as five hundred rafting trips from Redding to Anderson, involving more than two thousand passengers, many from afar. Business and other groups raft the river to build teamwork.

Some choose to go against the flow. One such individual is Garth Schmeck, who founded the Penguin Paddlers kayaking club in Redding, which grew to 700 members. Each year he usually paddles an improbable seventeen-foot sea kayak five or so miles up the Sacramento, not unlike a salmon's journey. Schmeck, who cites a tremendous "endorphin rush" from this invigorating challenge, then rewards himself with a relaxing trip back downriver, now going with the current.

Swimming

The Sacramento River presents few traditional swimming opportunities. The river from Redding to Red Bluff is too cold and dangerous for enjoyable swimming, other than for the hardy. Below Red Bluff the river becomes increasingly turbid with algae, sediment, runoff matter, and more.

Nevertheless, in 2011, one man decided

Extreme swimmer Jamie Patrick on his 111-mile swim from Princeton to Sacramento. Brian Hayes Patterson.

the river was perfect for a good swim—for 111 miles. That swimmer was Jamie Patrick, an "extreme open-water swimmer." Patrick looks at a globe and sees mainly water he wants to swim. In August of 2011, the forty-year-old San Francisco businessman entered the water at Princeton (above Colusa) and didn't leave it for more than thirty-one hours, arm-stroking all the way to Sacramento. He did this as a fundraiser to promote child literacy and to raise awareness about the importance of clean water. But he mainly did it to satisfy his life's craving—the challenge of an extreme swim.

Patrick reported that he was somewhat freaked out by the dozens of river otters that dove and surfaced close to him, as though trying to figure out what he was doing in their domain. (He had reason for concern: river otters are very territorial and have been known to attack a human.) Other wildlife—like egrets, herons, and geese—enthralled him throughout his journey.

He later wrote in his journal: "I saw and experienced this river like no one had before. For 31 hours I lived as an aquatic animal. I absorbed the river's culture and learned to speak its language. It became my home. There was no other place I would rather have been."

His concluding message: "If people take advantage of what this river offers, hopefully they'll take care of it."

Along the River

While some float on top or dive beneath a waterway's surface, others are content to travel alongside. Thoreau revealed a universal truth when he wrote, "Who hears the rippling of rivers will not utterly despair of anything. We go to the river's edge for comfort, spiritual renewal, meditation, solitude; we go to the river to feel and know the continuance of life."

People bond with the Sacramento River in many ways: walking, hiking, biking, rollerblading, horseback riding, meditating, picnicking, socializing, and more. When a river runs through a city—such as in Redding, split by the Sacramento—residents reap the blessings. One of the foremost trail networks in the country has been developed around the river there. It began in the early 1980s when the City Council approved a three-mile trail paralleling a defunct rail line alongside the river. Thus was born the "Sacramento River Trail."

In 1990, at the upper end of this trail, Redding built a footbridge spanning the river—a 418-foot stress-ribbon bridge, the first of its kind in North America. The trail continued down the river's other side, ending at the historic Diestelhorst Bridge to complete a six-mile elliptical route.

Under the direction of Bill Kuntz, the Bureau of Land Management transformed a former rail line from Keswick Dam to Shasta Dam into the "Sacramento River Rail Trail." (Such a trail is part of a nationwide effort to transform decommissioned rail lines into usable pathways for pedestrians and cyclists, called "Rails to Trails.") This nine-mile paved trail runs alongside Keswick Reservoir and is a favorite of cyclists. (Both it and the Sacramento River Trail have since been designated "National Recreational Trails.")

The River Trail is woven into the daily fabric of Redding life. Some residents walk, run, or rollerblade on the trail daily or weekly—often with dogs. Parents pull tots in bicycle carts or push them in strollers. Groups like the Sierra Club or California Native Plant Society organize events such as full-moon walks or strolls with an expert horticulturist. Bird watchers amble the trail with binoculars. Others may just sit on the river's bank, perhaps in a yoga pose or strumming a guitar.

A group that promotes walking is the Shasta

The Ribbon Bridge is part of the River Trail, connecting pathways on both sides of the river. Bob Madgic.

Cycling is popular on the River Trail. Here a couple includes their young child in a trailer on their ride. Bob Madgic.

Throughout the year many races are held on Redding's River Trail. Bob Madgic.

Shasta Sundial Strollers walk each week on one of the many trails along the Sacramento River. Bob Madgic.

The Nature Park at Anderson River Park is popular with equestrians. Bob Madgic.

Many community and recreational activities occur in Anderson River Park. Bob Madgic.

Sundial Strollers, an affiliate of the American Volkssport Association. (Volkssport began in Germany in the 1960s and is now a worldwide organization devoted to walking.) The Sacramento River—with its many pathways—is central to their weekly walking regimens. One member said, "If it wasn't for Shasta Sundial Strollers and our weekly river walks, I would stay at home and read, and never meet anybody. People seem to be happy when they're near the river, are more apt to smile and say hello."

One woman—Mandy—has been coming to the banks of the Sacramento River with her two dogs for months, extending to years. When asked why, she cites the power of water. "It's the force of life," she states. "This is where I find serenity; it's where my *chi* is restored. The flowing water cleanses my mind of clutter and fills my soul with peace and acceptance. I feel I belong here. It's my spiritual place."

Horseback riders also love to ride along the river's shores or on trails with vistas. One local rider finds the Sacramento very "horse friendly." She can bring her horse to the water's edge and let him step in for a cooling respite. She marvels at how the river changes from week to week, month to month, season by season. Its color, volume, configuration, and current often differ with each visit. And each time she comes to the river, she, too, is different, bringing with her that day's moods and thoughts. Greek philosopher Heraclitus stated this truth: "No man ever steps in the same river twice, for it's not the same river and he's not the same man."

Another female rider says she always feels uplifted when she rides out to the Sacramento. One Easter Sunday she was alone without family and feeling quite depressed. She loaded her horse and saddle in the trailer and went to the trails in the Bend area. While riding, she saw displays of lupine, Indian paintbrush, Mariposa lily, larkspur, and brodiaea. She sighted colorful Lewis and acorn woodpeckers and western bluebirds. In the distance stood snow-capped Lassen Peak. She reached an overlook where the Sacramento makes a sweeping turn through masses of greenery. There she sat, ate some snacks, and absorbed her surroundings. Her horse provided companionship and comfort. Returning to the trailhead refreshed, she felt she had experienced the sentiments of a song sung at her church, "Nearer, my God, to thee."

Regardless of the activity—whether walking, biking, riding, or meditating—the ever-changing Sacramento River is always present, offering its gifts of consciousness, tranquility, and inspiration to whomever will listen and receive.

Iron Canyon and the Bend Area

A few miles north of Red Bluff, the "Bend Area" in Shasta and Tehama counties stands out for its rugged landscapes, natural beauty, and recreational opportunities. There the river encounters a hard-rock volcanic formation that channels it in a curving, twisting flow through vertical rock walls, lush riparian forests, and rolling oak woodlands and grasslands. Vernal pools that sparkle with carpets of yellow and white are interspersed throughout the area. Sweeping vistas await the hiker, equestrian, and mountain biker, often with colorful wildflowers in the foreground. The Bureau of Land Management owns and manages this land, much of the 17,000 acres acquired by buying or swapping parcels over a period of years.

This part of the valley is called Iron Canyon. Volcanoes left behind rock agglomerate that

The Bend area has several spectacular overlooks of the river. Bob Madgic.

The Yana Trail offers many vistas of the river, such as this one showing a drift boat slowly coming downstream. Bob Madgic.

over time metamorphosed into huge blocks of hard lava. These squeeze the river and create turbulent rapids at low flows and navigational hazards at high flows. It's why Red Bluff remained the head of navigation, despite numerous efforts—some involving dynamite—to "clean out" the channel above it of such hazards so as to allow boats to continue upriver to Redding.

In the 1940s, Congress approved a dam for Iron Canyon that would have backed the river as far up as the towns of Cottonwood and Anderson. Fortunately Congress didn't simultaneously approve the funds. Shasta County officials and residents vigorously fought the dam. Among their many reasons, it would

have ended salmon runs past the dam, stymieing Coleman National Fish Hatchery just as it was getting going.

So the region stayed intact and is properly touted today as a paradise for the outdoors person. The river offers fishing for trout, salmon, and steelhead; the lands can be hunted for mule deer, valley quail, wild pig, wild turkey, pheasant, and other small game. It's a wildflower and bird mecca. The rocks are coated and splotched with dazzling multi-colored lichens. And it's home to the most scenic trails in the entire Sacramento Valley.

The most prominent among the latter is the Yana Trail, named for the Native American tribe in the region. This eight-mile trail begins at Jellys Ferry at one end, or Perry Riffle at the other, and traces the river as it makes almost a 180-degree turn, actually flowing north in one place. The trail crosses riparian zones and small creeks, and traverses rolling blue oak savannah and lava rock formations. Traces of old Indian villages, hunting and fishing camps, stone tool workshops, and rock shelters reveal the region's human history.

About halfway along the Yana Trail, a short spur takes one to a massive rock outcropping that looks directly down on the river, as it bends east, then south, and finally west in a sweeping loop around Table Mountain. On a nearby shoreline is "Massacre Flat," site of a primitive campground used primarily by boaters. It is presumably named after a massacre of Yana Indians in 1864 after Indians killed two white

A champion of the Sacramento River and the Bend area is now-retired BLM official Kelly Williams, shown here leading trail workers. Marti Weidert.

The Bend area is a favorite place for horse people. Sherry Garvin.

Hikers on Jed's Overlook, now reachable by a trail. Bob Madgic.

women in Shasta County. Vengeful whites killed as many as five hundred Yana Indians, reducing their population to less than fifty.

Another stunning overlook is about a forty-minute easy trek from the Perry Riffle trailhead. There is usually a wildflower feast, most profuse from February through May. With generally open and level terrain, this overlook is very accommodating for picnicking, photographing, and more.

The dramatic natural features of this area, accompanied by its many recreational opportunities, caused senators Barbara Boxer and Dianne Feinstein in 2011 to submit a bill designating it the Sacramento River National Recreation Area. (Despite widespread support from local officials and diverse organizations, and the promise of federal dollars to manage the area, then-Congressman Wally Herger chose not to co-sponsor the bill. The bill remained dormant at the time of this book's publication.)

Few areas in any river setting deserve added protection and management support more than Iron Canyon and the Bend Area.

~

People choose to engage with the Sacramento River in untold ways. Some are content to let the river and its creatures be; others seek interaction with one or both.

The Sacramento River is a magnificent provider. Its water goes to distant places and quenches the thirst of countless people. But no one should deny that its prime purposes are to nurture the organisms that live in and near it, to sustain an invaluable ecosystem, and to offer its vast benefits to its human visitors.

The opening of Sundial Bridge, July 4, 2004. Michael Burke.

CHAPTER ELEVEN

River as Classroom

> *"Eventually, all things merge into one, and a river runs through it. The river was cut by the world's great flood and runs over rocks from the basement of time. On some of the rocks are timeless raindrops. Under the rocks are the words, and some of the words are theirs. I am haunted by waters."*
>
> *—Norman Maclean*

THE VALUES OF A NATURAL RIVER AND native species are today fully affirmed thanks to the elevation of ecological principles, the Clean Water and federal and state endangered species acts, and the many organizations and river champions dedicated to healthy waterways. In a never-ending process, however, each generation must learn anew and recommit to stewardship.

Most organizations involved with the Sacramento River, such as those discussed in Chapter Nine, have a strong educational component. In addition, fishing clubs, Audubon clubs, hiking and other outdoor groups, and conservation organizations—among many other entities—all seek to teach and inform on river stewardship.

Often the best teacher is the river itself.

The River as Teacher

Few learning experiences match seeing and doing firsthand. Many educational groups near the Sacramento take full advantage of this natural resource to help others learn. The Dunsmuir School District has taken students to the river coursing through town so they could learn about its ecology. Students collected insect and plant specimens, and released trout fry spawned from eggs they had nurtured in the classroom. The River Exchange holds river festivals and cleanup days to make citizens continually aware of the tremendous resource flowing nearby.

The Sacramento River Preservation Trust schedules raft trips and other river outings as its main teaching tool. It also organizes an annual "Snow Goose Festival," which includes numerous field trips to public and private entities dedicated to harmonious relationships with nature.

Another such "classroom" is the Sacramento River Discovery Center in Red Bluff. On-site environmental lessons are presented to students and other visiting groups. At summer camp, participants examine plants and rocks and wade in water to see what organisms live there. Thanks to a "stealth cam," students view activities of bobcats, beavers, coyotes, and other wildlife.

The Fly Shop's "Fish Camp" instructs youth in stream etymology and other fly fishing basics. Michael Caranci.

At the Center for Land-Based Learning in the town of Winters in Yolo County, students learn about the relationship between agriculture and watershed conservation. As part of the Student and Landowner Education and Watershed Stewardship (SLEWS) program, young people plant trees and other flora to restore riparian and wildlife habitat. Since 2001, more than seven hundred students have experienced this integrated learning of biological and ecological concepts. At the same time, they come to know and appreciate where they live and what's vital to sustain the watershed.

One school that uses the river as an integral part of its curriculum is the Chrysalis Charter School in Shasta County, a K–8 school that focuses on science and the environment. At the beginning of each school year, all 150 students raft down the river in groups. This activity,

High school students restore riparian vegetation through the SLEWS program based in Winters. Nick DiRienzo.

The River Exchange in Dunsmuir organizes a river cleanup each year that also targets invasive plants like Scotch broom shown here. Robin Singler.

At the Sacramento River Discovery Center in Red Bluff, youth collect water organisms for study. Bobie Hughes.

Redding's Chrysalis School begins each school year with a raft trip on the Sacramento. Bob Madgic.

according to school officials, helps to "build community and have students and teachers get better acquainted. Plus, it's fun!"

Chrysalis draws upon the Sacramento River watershed throughout the year so students can observe wildlife and fish and learn how rivers work. They examine what constitutes a watershed and where and how flows materialize. On rainy days, they may go outside to study erosion and flow patterns. They take weekly field trips to river-related locations such as the Coleman National Fish Hatchery.

Boy Scout troops throughout California travel to the Sacramento River to learn water and teamwork skills by canoeing and shore camping. Often, an older boy is placed with a younger one for mentoring. The river is an ideal training resource; it demands good navigational and paddling abilities.

Salmon become both curriculum and teacher in the "Return of the Salmon" festival held each October at the Coleman National Fish

It's important for boating safety to learn how to "read the water." Bob Madgic.

A popular, educational activity is having school children raise fish fry for release in natural waters. Provided by Shasta-Trinity Fly Fishers.

Hatchery in Shasta County. Visitors witness Chinook salmon fighting their way up man-made channels and small waterfalls to reach their spawning destination. Nothing rivals seeing these fish up close as they carry out their life's mission, their fierce determination and brute strength in full display. The hatchery instructs visitors on the life cycles of salmon—from eggs (which hatchery officials collect and spawn) to the salmon fry that are released back to the river.

The Battle Creek Salmon Trail runs from the hatchery to the California Department of Fish and Game's Battle Creek Wildlife Area. This two-mile trail, completed in 2010, passes wetland ponds, riparian foliage, and sections of Battle Creek, with signage identifying plants,

Students releasing fry into the river. Provided by Shasta-Trinity Fly Fishers.

birds, insects, and other natural features. Walkers may also see migrating salmon in the fall as they swim up Battle Creek to the Coleman hatchery.

State and federal wildlife refuges up and down the Sacramento Valley highlight wildlife viewing. One example is the Yolo Bypass Wildlife Area, a premier birding area for waterfowl, shorebirds, and raptors. Large numbers of warblers, tanagers, flycatchers, and other neotropical migrants can be seen in the riparian forests. Ground-nesting birds include ring-necked pheasants, mallards, and northern harriers.

The Yolo Basin Foundation and DFG co-host "Discover the Flyway," an educational outreach program focused on hands-on learning. More than three thousand students and parents participate in Flyway field trips each year. The foundation also conducts monthly tours to view evening bat flights.

Turtle Bay Exploration Park

The most encompassing complex devoted to learning about the Sacramento River is Redding's Turtle Bay Exploration Park. It presents a comprehensive, integrated river curriculum focusing on natural and human history, native plants, fishery, and wildlife. Ongoing exhibits—many of them interactive—feature topics ranging from energy conservation to water usage.

What has long made Turtle Bay a special place is its location.

As the Sacramento River courses through Redding, it plows into a vertical red wall of iron deposits and rocky cobble, producing a sweeping ninety-degree turn. Such a severe bend creates fast outer currents, eddies, backwaters, and a "bay." There the river deposits whatever it is carrying—gravel, minerals, sediment—creating a broad alluvial floodplain.

The Arboretum at Turtle Bay presents plants native to the five Mediterranean regions of the world. Bob Madgic.

The Turtle Bay Museum. Bob Madgic.

The location was special to the Wintu, who built one of their largest villages there. With low summer flows and an abundance of spring-run salmon, the Wintu spread a net across the shallow river and annually reaped a rich harvest. An abundance of mussels enriched their diet and also helped keep the water clean and pure.

Hordes of miners were also drawn to this spot in the mid-1800s. In their relentless quest for gold, they dispersed and annihilated the native people. To uncover the seductive metal, they dredged the river and excavated its banks. As late as 1917, they were using a contraption called a "doodlebug" to unearth ever-larger swaths of river gravel. Despite heaps of pilings left for future generations to clean up, little gold was actually taken from this site.

Loggers, too, were attracted to the region. Timber cut upriver was floated down and gathered in the bay. A sawmill got established. Workers noted how turtles—western pond turtles—emerged from their haunts and often sunned on the logs. They called this spot "turtle bay," and the lumber company named itself the Turtle Bay Sawmill.

In the mid-1900s, Benton Ranch sprouted up on the other side of the river. It grazed only a few sheep and cows and grew some grains. In the early 1980s, a development company purchased the property, intending to build a nine-hundred-home subdivision. But when the economy tanked, the company defaulted. A wealthy resident, Leah McConnell—co-founder of the McConnell Foundation with her husband, Carl, who died in 1985—purchased the land from the Benton Trust (where it had reverted) and then exchanged it for property the McConnells had previously donated to the

A popular Turtle Bay exhibit is the aquarium featuring native and introduced fishes of the Sacramento River watershed. Courtesy of Turtle Bay Exploration Park.

city. She also gave Redding over a million dollars, stipulating that approximately half was to be used for an arboretum.

In 1992, the McConnell Foundation bought the Benton property back from Redding, with the proviso the city use some of the money to build a pedestrian bridge across the river. It then leased the land to the newly formed "Shasta Natural Science Association" for an arboretum. The Shasta Natural Science Association (formerly Carter House Science Museum) was one of four entities that joined to form the "Alliance of Redding Museums." The others were the Arboretum, the Redding Museum of Art History, and a Forest Museum that existed only on paper.

From this alliance came a complex initially called "Turtle Bay Museums and Arboretum on the River," to be located at the dual properties straddling the river at the bay. These lands were badly degraded from mining and excavations, the disturbed gravel and heaps of tailings looking like a moonscape. Where vegetated, invasive exotics had replaced the native manzanita and ceanothus bushes. To attract grants, the alliance conceived an innovative museum concept: create an interdisciplinary complex incorporating human and natural history, science, and art, all linked to the nearby river. This integrated approach swayed several potential grantors, and the new "Turtle Bay Exploration Park" was launched.

First came the Turtle Bay Museum, which opened in 2002. Upon entering, a "wall of water" greets the visitor, symbolizing its importance for all that follows. A large aquarium features native watershed fish and introduced species. Historic re-creations of Native American and early pioneer life and many interactive activities offer informative and hands-on expe-

"Wings of Summer" is a seasonal exhibit at Turtle Bay's living Butterfly House. Bob Madgic.

riences. Special exhibits and programs rotate throughout the year.

The three-hundred-acre complex includes the Paul Bunyan Forest Camp, the forestry museum long sought for Shasta County. Modeled after an old-time forest camp, it features wildlife such as owls, eagles, hawks, snakes, and lizards for viewing and demonstrations.

Across the river is the McConnell Arboretum and Botanical Gardens—an expansion of the original arboretum. The twenty-acre gardens contain native plants from the five Mediterranean climate zones: central California west of the Sierra Nevada, Mediterranean Basin, South Africa, Chile, and Southern and Western Australia. There is also a children's garden, medicinal garden, butterfly garden, unique water displays, and other artistic creations.

A year round aviary exhibit at Turtle Bay is the Parrott Playhouse featuring Australian "lories" or "lorikeets." Bob Madgic.

Patriot and Liberty

I N THE fall of 2004, two eagles built a nest in a tall cottonwood tree in what is now the Bird Sanctuary of Turtle Bay. In the spring of 2006 two eaglets hatched. The eagle family was visible from a nearby highway bridge crossing the Sacramento River and soon became locally prominent. The Redding newspaper *Record Searchlight* held a contest to name the parents, and "Patriot" and "Liberty" were chosen.

Construction to enlarge the bridge began in early 2008. Since eagles are usually sensitive to any disturbances near their nesting site, the DFG asked the California Department of Transportation (Caltrans) to "encourage" the birds to nest elsewhere. To do this, tree climbers placed a large black cone over the nest when Patriot and Liberty were gone. When the eagle pair returned to their

"The Unstoppable Eagles," Liberty and Patriot. Terri Luillier.

original haunt to nest again, they swooped at the plastic cone to knock it away. This dive-bombing went on for days. When their efforts failed to dislodge the cone, the birds started building another nest near it. In the meantime, a group of eagle fans had materialized, led by local elementary science teacher Terri Lhuillier. Between the eagles' unwavering determination and vigorous community support, Caltrans decided to remove the cone, allowing the two eagles to move back into their home.

As bridge construction proceeded, the DFG required Caltrans to monitor the eagles to see if it was adversely affecting their nesting. To that end, Caltrans installed a video camera on an overhead branch. Turtle Bay Exploration Park agreed to house the equipment and put the broadcast on its public web site.

It was soon apparent Patriot (male) and Liberty (female) were not fazed at all by the work just one hundred feet away, which included huge cranes, ear-splitting jack-hammering and excavating machinery, bright lights at night, and streams of start-and-go traffic. In late March, they hatched two eaglets, a televised event. "Conehead" and "Freedom" were chosen as names for the two new chicks.

The next closely followed event was the eaglets first leaving the nest—this typically occurs after about twelve weeks—and hopping from branch to branch in nervous pre-flight exercise called "branching." If all goes well, this is followed by the momentous "fledge," when an eagle takes its first significant flight beyond a few wing flaps. To celebrate and witness this successful happening, eagle enthusiasts organized a "fledgefest."

Patriot and Liberty were not done with displays of their prowess. The following year, they returned and laid three eggs, a rarity for eagles. A more sophisticated "Eaglecam" system had been set up, and across seven days it televised the laying of each egg. All three eaglets hatched and fledged (named "Spirit," "Hope," and "Freedom"), something only five percent of eagles ever achieve.

As if this weren't enough, the next year, 2010, Patriot and Liberty again produced and successfully fledged three eaglets. Schoolchildren voted for the names "Shasta," "Peace," and "Justice." In 2011, two more eaglets were born during a very blustery and rainy nesting season. Appropriately named "Stormy and "Windy," the chicks survived fierce winds, rain, and hail. By that spring, Patriot and Liberty had hatched and fledged eleven eaglets (one had occurred before all of the attention), almost unheard of by bald eagle couples—they mate for life—and all taking place in their notorious nest. More than a million people have viewed activities on the Eaglecam. Fledgefests have become annual events for each new brood of eaglets.

Teacher Terri Luillier uses the story of Liberty and Patriot in her classroom with a book she and her sister wrote and illustrated. Katie Zulliger.

"Cricket," a common barn owl, flies over the audience in Turtle Bay's "Walk on the Wild Side Animal Show."
Courtesy of Turtle Bay Exploration Park

The centerpiece of Turtle Bay is the Sundial Bridge—the pedestrian bridge Leah McConnell requested to link both sides of the river. But never could she have imagined such a bridge. Opened in 2004, the free-standing span consists of a 217-foot pylon with streaming cables—like harp strings—connected to an aqua-green, opaque glass deck. It is also a real sundial, telling time by the pylon's shadow on marked hours of the day along a tile-covered garden border. This creative masterpiece was designed by world-renowned Spanish architect Santiago Calatrava. To him, the bridge "resembles a bird in flight, and symbolizes the overcoming of adversity."

Visitors worldwide visit this stunning feature. Both daytime and nighttime walks are a special experience. The bridge has become a popular spot for organized walks and runs, among other events. Salmon and other fish can be spotted in the river below. A rich array of birds is always visible. Anglers often pass slowly by in a boat. The bridge links people with the river in tangible and intangible ways.

Turtle Bay continues to enhance its natural areas by restoring native plants and trees. At the end of 2009, the city of Redding hired River Partners to restore a seventy-six-acre riverside parcel on the property, an impenetrable mass of Himalayan blackberry bushes and other undesirable vegetation. A thousand goats were enlisted to chew up the foliage. Machinery downed the unwanted trees and cleared the remaining woody debris and roots, leaving just large cottonwood and oak trees. The team then planted nearly five thousand plants, including native blackberry bushes, along with thirty thousand plugs of native grasses. The result is a revitalized "Bird Sanctuary," intersected by a walking trail. Birdsong stations along the trail invite walkers to push buttons to hear the sounds of neighboring birds.

Two birds that have been visible several months each year high in a nearby tree became famous. Bald eagles Patriot and Liberty could still be spotted from Turtle Bay's walking trails and from adjacent Highway 44 in 2012.

On September 23, 2011, the Sundial Bridge served as a metaphor in a global event—350.org's Moving Planet day of action—to encourage the use of energy sources other than fossil fuels. In Redding, a chain of participants walked 1.9 miles along a major traffic thoroughfare, before turning toward the Sundial Bridge. The walkers crossed the span to an area rich with riparian foliage and gardens and something generated by the sun—a huge sundial. The symbolic and educational message could not have been clearer. As event organizer Peggy Rebol stated: "We wanted to leave the freeway and cars and get to the other side of the bridge, where we have clean, renewable, sustainable energy."

~

What makes all of this possible is the river running through it.

Bridge crossing: 350.org's Moving Planet Day of Action, September 23, 2011. Bob Madgic.

A red shouldered hawk enriches river vistas. Bob Madgic.

Epilogue

FROM OUR HOME OVERLOOKING THE Sacramento River, I observe the waterway's countless images. I often wade its waters. Across several years, I note changes: more eroded banks; a deepened channel on one side and a shallower bend on the other from added gravel and silt deposits; more mayfly than caddis hatches. The river's flows fluctuate from month to month, year to year, depending on rainfall, the varying levels presenting different sights, sounds, and processes.

I don't see as many salmon as in years past and sorely miss their acrobatic jumps. Spawning redds in this part of the river have been sparse. In earlier years, bald eagles, vultures, otters, and the like feasted on plentiful salmon carcasses, which are now in short supply. Eagles still fly the river corridor along with many other birds—osprey, hawks, geese, ducks, kingfishers, egrets, great blue herons—all of which keep the scene rich and highly stimulating.

Normal river behavior accounts for some of these changes. But others are the result of human interference, a dominant pattern for two hundred years. It's gratifying that several groups have launched ambitious efforts to restore some of what has been lost.

The issues impacting the Sacramento River persist. Residential areas keep expanding on what used to be floodplain, so concerns and posited solutions about flood protection are ongoing. The unreliable levees along the river and throughout the Delta must get fixed. The costs will be huge, but no other alternative exists. Humans are here to stay in the Sacramento Valley. Many, many people beyond the valley depend on what happens here.

Despite the naysayers, climate change is heightening all issues.

The most vexing ones have been and continue to be over water. No one should question that what's best for the river, estuary, ocean, and the flora and fauna that occupy these realms is for the Sacramento to retain all water coming into it from all sources. Each attempt to divert more water compromises the natural river. Every loss of habitat, whether aquatic or riparian, means fewer places for wildlife. Past alterations have had dramatic consequences, such as the decline of salmon and other native species.

Above all, a healthy human race calls for thriving river ecosystems.

Yet attempts to manipulate the river continue. To create more water storage, planning is underway to raise Shasta Dam. So, too, is a reincarnation of a peripheral canal—twin "water tunnels"—to have river water bypass the Delta and go directly to the Central Valley. The arguments that agricultural and urban growth requires more water are hard to resist.

No simple answer or revolutionary technology exists to solve these longstanding problems. When the Sacramento River's integrity was intact, it gave rise to one of the richest biological regions in the world. Humans managed to engineer it down to a fraction of what it once was.

A river as transcendent as the Sacramento has an unlimited ability to restore and sustain itself. It really comes down to whether people possess the will to abide by Aldo Leopold's proposed land ethic "where lands and organisms are treated as a 'community,' and humans act to preserve its integrity, stability, and beauty.... Such an ethic changes the role of Homo sapiens from conqueror of the land-community to plain member and citizen of it."

The issue has been aptly framed by nineteenth-century Japanese conservationist Tanako Shozo: "The care of rivers is not a question of rivers, but of the human heart."

Bringing a Sacramento rainbow to the net. Allan Craig.

Bibliography

Alzueta, Carlos. "Iron Canyon," in *The Covered Wagon, 1992.* Shasta Historical Society.

Avella, Steven M. *Sacramento: Indomitable City.* San Francisco: Arcadia Publishing, 2003.

Ballenger, Craig Graham. *Shasta's Headwaters: An Angler's Guide to the Upper Sacramento and McCloud Rivers.* Portland: Frank Amato Publications, 1998.

Berry, Thomas. *The Dream of the Earth.* San Francisco: Sierra Club Books, 1988.

Bloom, Khaled J. *Murder of a Landscape: The California Farmer-Smelter War 1897-1916.* Norman, Oklahoma: The Arthur H. Clark Company, 2010.

Behnke, Robert J. *Trout and Salmon of North America.* New York: The Free Press, 2002.

Black, Michael. "Tragic Remedies: A Century of Failed Fishery Policy on California's Sacramento River." *Pacific Historical Review,* February, 1995.

California Rivers: A Public Trust Report. California Lands Commission, 1993.

California Trout. *Streamkeeper's Log,* Summer 2012.

Cushing, Colbert E. and J. David Allan. *Streams: Their Ecology and Life.* San Diego: Academic Press, 2001.

Dadigan, Marc, *California Watch,* September, 2011.

Dana, Julian. *The Sacramento: River of Gold.* New York: Farrar & Rinehart, 1939.

Doyle, Brian. "The Creature Beyond the Mountains." *Orion Magazine,* September-October, 2011.

Egan, Timothy. *The Good Rain: Across Time and Terrain in the Pacific Northwest.* New York: Alfred A. Knopf, 1990.

Grosz, Terry. *Slaughter in the Sacramento Valley.* Boulder, CO: Johnson Books, 2009.

Haig-Brown, Roderick L. *A River Never Sleeps.* New York: Nick Lyons Books, 1974.

Hart, John and David Sanger. *San Francisco Bay: Portrait of an Estuary.* Berkeley: University of California Press, 2003.

Heiser, Robert F. Editor. *Handbook of North American Indians,* Volume Eight, California. Washington, D.C.: Smithsonian Institution, 1978.

Hesse, Herman. *Siddharha.* New York: New Directions Publishing Corporation, 1951.

Hildebrandt, William R., and Michael J. Darcangelo. *Life on the River.* Berkeley: Heyday Books, 2008.

Hoveman, Alice R., with contributions by Frank LaPena, Elaine Sundahl and Ronald M. Yoshiyama. *Journey to Justice: The Wintu People and the Salmon.* Redding: Turtle Bay Exploration Park, 2002.

Hundley, Jr. Norris. *The Great Thirst: Californians and Water, 1770s-1990s.* Berkeley: University of California Press, 1992.

Jenkins, Matt. "Breakdown, 'The Cadillac of California irrigation districts' has more than a tiny fish to blame for its trouble," in *High Country News,* January 11, 2010.

Johnson, Stephen, Gerald Haslam and Robert Dawson. *The Great Central Valley.* Berkeley: University of California Press, 1993.

Johnson, Arthur T. *California: An Englishman's Impressions of the Golden State.* London: S. Paul & Co. 1913.

Kelley, Robert. *Battling The Inland Sea.* Berkeley: University of California Press, 1989.

Lawson, John D. *Redding & Shasta County: Gateway to the Cascades.* Northridge: Windsor Publications, 1986.

Lewis, Oscar. *The Sacramento River.* New York: Holt, Rinehart and Winston, 1970.

Lufkin, Alan. Editor. *Salmon and Steelhead: The Struggle to Restore an Imperiled Resource.* Berkeley: University of California Press, 1991.

Madgic, Bob. *A Guide to California's Freshwater Fishes.* Happy Camp: Naturegraph Publications, 1999.

Margolin, Malcolm. *The Way We Lived.* Berkeley: Heyday Books, 1981.

Martens, Tom. "Delta Stripers Threatened," in *California Fly Fisher,* February, 2012.

Masson, Marcelle. *A Bag of Bones.* Happy Camp: Naturegraph Publications, 1966.

Mazariegos, Darla Greb. *Images of America: Mount Shasta.* San Francisco: Arcadia Publishing Company, 2007.

McGinnis, Samuel M. *Freshwater Fishes of California.* Berkeley: University of California Press, 1984.

Miesse, William C. and Robyn G. Peterson. *Sudden and Solitary: Mount Shasta and Its Artistic Legacy, 1841-2008.* Berkeley: Heyday Books, 2008.

"Modern Salmon and the Ice Age: Salmon Life History is Tested First by Mountain Building, then Ice." Marine Biology and Oceanography @ *Suite 101.*

Moore, Kathleen Dean. *Riverwalking: Reflections on Moving Water.* New York: Harcourt Brace & Company, 1995.

Moyle, Peter B. *Inland Fishes of California.* Berkeley: University of California Press, 2002.

Muir, John, editor. *West of the Rocky Mountains.* Philadelphia: Running Press, 1888.

Neasham, V. Aubrey. *Wild Legacy: California Hunting and Fishing Tales.* Berkeley: Howell-North Books, 1973.

Norman, Seth. "Bats and Other Mercies." In *California Fly Fisher,* February, 2012.

O'Brien, Chip. *River Journal: Sacramento River.* Portland: Frank Amato Publications, 1997.

Palmer, Tim. *Stanislaus: The Struggle for a River.* Berkeley: University of California Press, 1982.

Petersen, David. *On the Wild Edge.* New York: Henry Holt and Company, 2005.

Powers, Stephen. *Tribes of California.* Berkeley: University of California Press, 1976.

Reisner, Marc. *Cadillac Desert: The American West and its Disappearing Water.* New York: Penguin Books, 1987.

Rocca, Al M. *America's Shasta Dam: A History of Construction, 1936-1945.* Renown Publishing Company, 1994.

Rocca, Al M. *Shasta Lake: Boomtowns and the Building of Shasta Dam.* San Francisco: Arcadia Publishing, 2002.

Rodriguez, Richard. *Brown: The Last Discovery of America.* New York: Viking Penguin, 2003.

Sanders, Scott Russell. "Buffalo Eddy," in *Orion Magazine,* March/April, 2012.

"Salmon Crisis." *Outdoor California,* July-August, 2009.

Schoenherr, Allan A. *A Natural History of California.* Berkeley: University of California, 1992.

Sisk, Coleen. Tribal Chieftain, Winnemem Wintu Tribe. Interviews. Redding, 2006.

Simmons, Edward. *From Seven to Seventy: Memories of a Painter and a Yankee.* New York: Harper, 1922.

Smith, Dottie. *The Dictionary of Early Shasta County History,* 1999.

Stegner, Wallace. *Where the Bluebird Sings to the Lemonade Springs.* New York: Wings Books, 1992.

Steinhart, Peter. *California's Wild Heritage: Threatened and Endangered Animals in the Golden State.* California Department of Fish and Game, California Academy of Sciences, Sierra Club Books, 1990.

White, Thelma B. "The Many Facets of the Sacramento River," in *Ripples Along Chico Creek,* National League of American Pen Women, Butte County Branch, 1992.